CW00326861

# Ovid

Selected by
David Hopkins

PHOENIX
POETRY

This edition first published by Everyman in 1998
Phoenix edition first published in 2003

Selection and glossary © J. M. Dent 1998
Chronology © J. M. Dent 2003

ISBN 0 75381 748 9

Typeset by Deltatype Ltd, Birkenhead, Merseyside
Printed in China by South China Printing Co. Ltd.

A CIP catalogue reference for this book
is available from the British Library.

The Orion Publishing Group
Orion House
5 Upper St Martin's Lane
London
WC2H 9EA

The translations from Ovid included in this selection are
taken from versions by English poets of the late seventeenth
and early eighteenth centuries. These were chosen because
they convey the feel and flavour of Ovid's witty style more
vividly than any other English translations.

# Contents

Ovid

# from *Amores* ('Loves')

## 1.1

*How Ovid came to write love elegies.*

For mighty wars I thought to tune my lute,
And make my measures to my subject suit.
Six feet for every verse the Muse designed,
But Cupid, laughing, when he saw my mind,
From every second verse a foot purloined.
Who gave thee, boy, this arbitrary sway,
Or subjects not thy own commands to lay,
Who Phoebus only and his laws obey?
'Tis more absurd than if the queen of love
Should in Minerva's arms to battle move,
Or manly Pallas from that queen should take
Her torch, and o'er the dying lover shake.
In fields as well may Cynthia sow the corn,
Or Ceres wind in woods the bugle horn.
As well may Phoebus quit the trembling string
For sword and shield, and Mars may learn to sing.
Already thy dominions are too large;
Be not ambitious of a foreign charge!
If thou wilt reign o'er all, and everywhere,
The god of music for his harp may fear.
Thus when with soaring wings I seek renown,
Thou pluck'st my pinions, and I flutter down.
Could I on such mean thoughts my Muse employ,
I want a mistress, or a blooming boy.
Thus I complained; his bow the stripling bent,
And chose an arrow fit for his intent.
The shaft his purpose fatally pursues;
'Now, poet, there's a subject for thy Muse,'
He said – too well, alas, he knows his trade!

For in my breast a mortal wound he made.
Far hence, ye proud hexameters remove,
My verse is paced and trammelled into love.
With myrtle wreaths my thoughtful brows enclose,
While in unequal verse I sing my woes.

## 1.4

*Ovid instructs his mistress on how to behave at a feast, with her husband present.*

Your husband will be with us at the treat:
May that be the last supper he shall eat!
And am poor I a guest invited there,
Only to see, while he may touch, the fair?
To see you kiss and hug your nauseous lord,
While his lewd hand descends below the board?
Now wonder not that Hippodamia's charms
At such a sight the centaurs urged to arms;
That in a rage they threw their cups aside,
Assailed the bridegroom, and would force the bride.
I am not half a horse – I would I were! –
Yet hardly can from you my hands forbear.
Take, then, my counsel, which, observed, may be
Of some importance both to you and me.
Be sure to come before your man be there;
There's nothing can be done, but come howe'er.
Sit next him – that belongs to decency –
But tread upon my foot in passing by;
Read in my looks what silently they speak,
And slyly with your eyes your answer make.
My lifted eyebrow shall declare my pain;
My right hand to his fellow shall complain,
And on the back a letter shall design,

Besides a note that shall be writ in wine.
Whene'er you think upon our last embrace,
With your forefinger gently touch your face;
If any word of mine offend my dear,
Pull, with your hand, the velvet of your ear;
If you are pleased with what I do or say,
Handle your rings, or with your fingers play;
As suppliants use at altars, hold the board,
Whene'er you wish the devil may take your lord.
When he fills for you, never touch the cup,
But bid th' officious cuckold drink it up.
The waiter on those services employ;
Drink you, and I will snatch it from the boy,
Watching the part where your sweet mouth hath been,
And thence with eager lips will suck it in.
If he with clownish manners thinks it fit
To taste, and offer you the nasty bit,
Reject his greasy kindness, and restore
Th' unsavoury morsel he had chewed before;
Nor let his arms embrace your neck, nor rest
Your tender cheek upon his hairy breast;
Let not his hand within your bosom stray,
And rudely with your pretty bubbies play;
But, above all, let him no kiss receive:
That's an offence I never can forgive!
Do not, O do not, that sweet mouth resign,
Lest I rise up in arms and cry, ''Tis mine!'
I shall thrust in betwixt, and, void of fear,
The manifest adulterer will appear.
These things are plain to sight; but more I doubt
What you conceal beneath your petticoat.
Take not his leg between your tender thighs,
Nor with your hand provoke my foe to rise.

How many love-inventions I deplore,
Which I myself have practised all before!
How oft have I been forced the robe to lift
In company; to make a homely shift
For a bare bout, ill huddled o'er in haste,
While o'er my side the fair her mantle cast!
You to your husband shall not be so kind;
But, lest you should, your mantle leave behind.
Encourage him to tope, but kiss him not,
Nor mix one drop of water in his pot.
If he be fuddled well, and snores apace,
Then we may take advice from time and place.
When all depart, when compliments are loud,
Be sure to mix among the thickest crowd;
There I will be, and there we cannot miss,
Perhaps to grubble, or at least to kiss.
Alas, what length of labour I employ,
Just to secure a short and transient joy!
For night must part us; and when night is come,
Tucked underneath his arm he leads you home.
He locks you in; I follow to the door,
His fortune envy, and my own deplore.
He kisses you, he more than kisses too;
Th' outrageous cuckold thinks it all his due.
But add not to his joy by your consent,
And let it not be giv'n, but only lent.
Return no kiss, nor move in any sort;
Make it a dull and a malignant sport.
Had I my wish, he should no pleasure take,
But slubber o'er your business for my sake;
And whate'er fortune shall this night befall,
Coax me tomorrow, by forswearing all.

(trans. John Dryden)

## 1.5

*Ovid's mistress comes to him at siesta-time.*

'Twas noon, when I, scorched with the double fire
Of the hot sun and my more hot desire,
Stretched on my downy couch at ease was laid,
Big with expectance of the lovely maid.
The curtains but half-drawn, a light let in,
Such as in shades of thickest groves is seen;
Such as remains, when the sun flies away,
Or when night's gone, and yet it is not day.
This light to modest maids must be allowed,
Where shame may hope its guilty head to shroud.
And now my love, Corinna, did appear,
Loose on her neck fell her divided hair;
Loose as her flowing gown, that wantoned in the air.
In such a garb, with such a grace and mien,
To her rich bed came th' Assyrian queen.
So Lais looked, when all the youth of Greece
With adoration did her charms confess.
Her envious gown to pull away I tried,
But she resisted still, and still denied;
But so resisted, that she seemed to be
Unwilling to obtain the victory.
So I at last an easy conquest had,
Whilst my fair combatant herself betrayed:
But when she naked stood before my eyes,
Gods, with what charms did she my soul surprise!
What snowy arms did I both see and feel!
With what rich globes did her soft bosom swell!
Plump as ripe clusters rose each glowing breast,
Courting the hand, and suing to be pressed!
What a smooth plain was on her belly spread,
Where thousand little loves and graces played!

What thighs! What legs! But why strive I in vain,
Each limb, each grace, each feature, to explain?
One beauty did through her whole body shine.
I saw, admired, and pressed it close to mine.
The rest, who knows not? Thus entranced we lay,
Till in each other's arms we died away.
O give me such a noon, ye gods, to every day!

(trans. Richard Duke)

## 1.13

*Ovid begs the morning not to come too swiftly.*

Aurora, rising from old Tithon's bed,
Does o'er the eastern skies her roses spread;
Stay, beauteous Morn, awhile thy chariot stay,
Awhile with lagging wheels retard the day!
So may young birds, as often as the spring
Renews the year, o'er Memnon's ashes sing.
Now I lie folded in Corinna's arms,
And all her soul is mine, and all her charms.
I now am to her panting bosom pressed,
And now, if ever lover was, am blessed.
As yet sweet sleep sits heavy on your eyes,
And warbling birds forbid, as yet, to rise.
Stay, beauteous Morning! For to lovesick maids
And youths, how grateful are these dusky shades!
Ah stay, and do not from the blushing east,
With dawning glories break our balmy rest.
When Night's black mantle does those glories hide,
The pilot by the stars his ship can guide,
And in mid-sea a certain course pursue,
As safe as when he has thy sun in view.
What pleasure in thy light should mortals take?

Thou dost the weary traveller awake;
Though to the down his heavy head reclines,
Up he must lift it, for the morning shines.
The soldier braces on his brazen shield,
Quits his warm tent, and fits him for the field.
The labouring hind his harrow takes, and now
The peasant yokes his oxen to the plough.
The boy, half-waked and rubbing still his eyes,
Is loath alike to go to school or rise;
While o'er his task he does imperfect nod,
He fears the ferula, he dreads the rod.
The bridegroom, starting from his bride's embrace,
Runs to his lawyer to consult his case;
A word is wanting in the dower deed;
And what, to save the portion, must he plead?
Now hungry sergeants quit their tempting ease,
To haunt the crowded courts and pick up fees.
Thy rise brings labour to the female band,
And puts the spindle in the spinster's hand.
Light are these toils, and little is the pain
To rise to work, and rest at night again.
But who that e'er knew love's transporting joys,
Could from the arms of youth and beauty rise?
Oft have I wished that night would keep her ground,
And all her stars be at thy rising found.
Oft have I wished the winds would stop thy way,
Repel thy car, or clouds involve the day.
Dost thou in envy lash each lazy steed,
And whirl thy chariot with unwonted speed?
Black was thy son, and in his hue's expressed
The gloomy passions of his parent's breast.
He, born of Cephalus, his ravished sire,
Is a known proof of thy adulterous fire.
Thou, by his colour, wouldst thy crime conceal:

Ah, that to Tithon I the tale could tell!
Search all the records of heaven's lecher's round,
A fouler story cannot there be found.
In Cephalus' embraces when you lay,
And oft, by theft, renewed your wanton play:
When Tithon's impotence you made your sport,
Did you not think the joyous moments short?
Locked in his arms did you in transports lie,
Ah, would you not, like me, to Phoebus cry,
'Stop, stop, thy rapid course!' Am I to blame
That Tithon's old, and cannot feel thy flame?
See how the Moon does her Endymion keep
In night concealed, and drowned in dewy sleep!
As lovely as the Moon, as fair as thou,
Who freely where she loves her favours does bestow.
Jove, when he robbed Amphitryon of his joy,
Did two whole nights in amorous thefts employ.
Unknown, when in Alcmena's arms he lay,
The night he doubles, and suspends the day.

  The morning heard my railing, and for shame
Blushed, that by force she must disturb my flame.
Bright Phoebus rushing forth, the glorious day
Drove the dear shades that hid our joys away.


## 3.7

*Ovid laments an 'imperfect enjoyment'.*

Was she not heavenly fair, and rich attired?
Was she not that which all my soul desired?
Yet were these arms around her idly spread,
And with a useless load I pressed the bed.
Ev'n to my wishes was the power denied,
When with my wishes the kind nymph complied.

I lay without life's animated spring,
A dull, enervate, worthless, lumpish thing.
My neck she folded with a soft embrace,
Now kissed my eyes, now wantoned o'er my face,
Now loved to dart her humid tongue to mine,
Now would her pliant limbs around me twine,
And soothe, by thousand ways, the sweet design.
The moving blandishments of sound she tried,
And, 'My dear life, my soul, my all!' she cried.
In vain, alas, the nerves were slackened still,
And I proved only potent in my will.
A poor, unactive sign of man I made,
And might as well, for use, have been a shade.
If old I live, how shall I old prevail,
When in my youth I thus inglorious fail?
The bloom of years becomes my shameful moan,
Now in full growth the ripened man is shown,
But not the strength of man to her was known.
Untouched by brothers, sisters thus retire,
Or Vestals rise to watch th' eternal fire.
Yet many a nymph, whom I forbear to name,
Have kindly yielded, and indulged my flame,
Nor could the vigour of their Ovid blame.
Corinna knows, when numbering the delight,
Not less than nine full transports crowned the night.
Is verse, or herbs, the source of present harms?
Am I captive to Thessalian charms?
Has some enchantress this confusion brought,
And in soft wax my tortured image wrought?
Deep in the liver is the needle fixed?
Plagues she by numbers, or by juices mixed?
By numbers, sudden the ripe harvests die,
And fruitful urns no more their streams supply:
Oaks shed, unshook, their acorns at the call,

And the vine wonders why her clusters fall.
Why may not magic act on me the same,
Unstring the nerves, and quite untune the frame?
Galled at the heart, and longing to perform,
I raised indeed, but raised an empty storm;
Most disappointed, when the most propense,
And shame was second cause of impotence.
What limbs I touched, and only touched! O fie!
Where was the blissful touch? Her shift can vie
In feats, like these, and touch as well as I.
Yet to touch her, ev'n Nestor might grow young,
And centuries, like twenty-one, be strung.
Such was the maid, the parallel had ran
Graceful, if I could add, such was the man.
Some envious deity with vengeance glowed,
So sweet a gift had been so ill bestowed.
I burned to clasp her naked in my arms,
Did she not freely open all her charms?
What boots good fortune, if we want the power
To snatch the pleasures of the favoured hour?
I, like a miser, only could behold,
And brooded o'er a useless mine of gold.
So Tantalus, with fruit untouched, is cursed,
And dies, amid the gliding stream, of thirst.
So rises early from th' untasted fair,
The grave old prelate, and kneels down to prayer.
Were yet her melting kisses misemployed?
Did she strive vainly to be well enjoyed?
Sure she has beauties might deaf rocks enchant,
Bend the proud oak, and soften adamant.
She would have moved a man, though almost dead,
But with my manhood the whole life was fled.
If none should lend an ear, why is the song?
Or painted nymphs shown to a blinded throng?

Ye gods, what joys did not my fancy raise!
I curled in folds of love a thousand ways.
Strong were my thoughts, but, ah, my body lay
Languid as roses plucked off yesterday.
Now all the blood the circling spirits fire,
And the lost field impertinent require:
Begone, untimely nerves! I trust no more:
Such was the promise of your strength before.
Could you the fair one balk of her delight,
Disgrace your master by so base a fright,
And want the courage for so sweet a fight?
Did she not kindly to your stay demand,
And tempt it softly with a soothing hand?
But when solicitings no life could gain,
And inspirations, though from her, were vain:
'Who bade thee thus thyself to me to bring?
Go, for a silly, unperforming thing!
Art thou a wretch, by some cursed spell destroyed,
Or here com'st fribbling, with past pleasures cloyed?'
  She spoke, and springing from the bed she flew,
And secret beauties so disclosed to view;
Yet to conceal the joyless night's disgrace,
She called for water, with a smiling face,
And washed a nameless, unpolluted, place.

(trans. anon., 1725)

13

# from Heroides ('Epistles of the Heroines')

## from 10: Ariadne to Theseus

*Ariadne, having helped Theseus to escape the Minotaur, is abandoned by her lover on the island of Naxos. She laments her desertion.*

When morning dew on all the fields did fall,
And birds with early songs for day did call,
Then I, half sleeping, stretched me towards your place,
And sought to press you with a new embrace,
Oft sought to press you close, but still in vain:
My folding arms came empty back again.
Startled, I rose, and found that you were gone,
Then on my widowed bed fell raging down;
Beat the fond breast, where, spite of me, you dwell,
And tore that hair which you once liked so well.
By the moon's light I the wide shore did view,
But all was desert, and no sight of you.
Then every way with love's mad haste I fly,
But ill my feet with my desires comply;
Weary they sink in the deep, yielding sands,
Refusing to obey such wild commands.
To all the shore of Theseus I complain:
The hills and rocks send back that name again;
Oft they repeat aloud the mournful noise,
And kindly aid a hoarse and dying voice.

  Though faint, yet still impatient, next I try
To climb a rough steep mountain which was nigh:
My furious love unusual strength supplied;
From thence, casting my eyes on every side,
Far off the flying vessel I espied.
In your swelled sails the wanton winds did play
(They court you, since they see you false as they);
I saw, or fancied that I saw you there,

And my chill veins froze up with cold despair;
Thus did I languish, till returning rage
In new extremes did my fired soul engage.
'Theseus,' I cry, 'perfidious Theseus, stay!'
But you are deaf, deaf as the winds, or sea!
'Stay your false flight, and let your vessel bear
Hence the whole number which she landed here!'
In loud and doleful shrieks I tell the rest;
And with fresh fury wound my hated breast.
Then all my shining ornaments I tear,
And with stretched arms wave them in open air,
That you might see her whom you could not hear.

(trans. Lord Somers)


## from 16: Paris to Helen

*Paris, visiting Sparta with the purpose of abducting Helen, tells her how*
*she was promised to him by the goddess Venus.*

A place there is in Ida's thickest grove
With oaks and fir trees shaded all above;
The grass here grows untouched by bleating flocks,
Or mountain goat, or the laborious ox.
From hence Troy's towers, magnificence and pride,
Leaning against an aged oak, I spied,
When straight, methought, I heard the trembling ground
With the strange noise of trampling feet resound.
In the same instant, Jove's great messenger,
On all his wings borne through the yielding air,
Lighting before my wondering eyes did stand;
His golden rod shone in his sacred hand.
With him three charming goddesses there came,
Juno and Pallas, and the Cyprian dame.
With an unusual fear I stood amazed,

Till thus the god my sinking courage raised:
'Fear not: thou art Jove's substitute below,
The prize of heavenly beauty to bestow;
Contending goddesses appeal to you;
Decide their strife.' He spake, and up he flew.
Then, bolder grown, I throw my fears away,
And every one with curious eyes survey.
Each of 'em merited the victory,
And I, their doubtful judge, was grieved to see
That one must have it, when deserved by three.
But yet that one there was which most prevailed,
And with more powerful charms my heart assailed.
Ah, would you know who thus my breast could move?
Who could it be but the fair queen of love?
With mighty bribes they all for conquest strive,
Juno will empires, Pallas valour give,
Whilst I stand doubting which I should prefer,
Empire's soft ease, or glorious toils of war;
But Venus gently smiled, and thus she spake:
'They're dangerous gifts, O do not, do not take!
I'll make thee love's immortal pleasures know,
And joys that in full tides for ever flow:
For, if you judge the conquest to be mine,
Fair Leda's fairer daughter shall be thine.'
She spake, and I gave her the conquest, due
Both to her beauty, and her gift of you.

(trans. Richard Duke)

## from 17: Helen to Paris

*Helen replies to Paris.*

Some right you claim, since naked to your eyes
Three goddesses disputed beauty's prize;
One offered valour, t' other crowns; but she
Obtained her cause, who, smiling, promised me.
But first I am not of belief so light
To think such nymphs would show you such a sight;
Yet granting this, the other part is feigned;
A bribe so mean your sentence had not gained.
With partial eyes I should myself regard,
To think that Venus made me her reward.
I humbly am content with human praise;
A goddess's applause would envy raise.
But be it as you say; for, 'tis confessed,
The men who flatter highest, please us best.
That I suspect it, ought not to displease;
For miracles are not believed with ease.
One joy I have, that I had Venus' voice;
A greater yet, that you confirmed her choice;
That proffered laurels, promised sovereignty,
Juno and Pallas, you contemned for me.
Am I your empire, then, and your renown?
What heart of rock, but must by this be won?
And yet bear witness, O you powers above,
How rude I am in all the arts of love!
My hand is yet untaught to write to men;
This is th' essay of my unpractised pen.
Happy those nymphs, whom use has perfect made!
I think all crime, and tremble at a shade.
Ev'n while I write, my fearful, conscious eyes
Look often back, misdoubting a surprise.
For now the rumour spreads among the crowd,

At court in whispers, but in town aloud.
Dissemble you, whate'er you hear 'em say:
To leave off loving were your better way;
Yet if you will dissemble it, you may.
  (trans. John Sheffield, Earl of Mulgrave, and John Dryden)

# from *Ars amatoria* ('The Art of Love')

## from Book 1

(1)

*The theatre and chariot race as places for amatory assignations.*

But, above all, the playhouse is the place;
There's choice of quarry in that narrow chase.
There take thy stand, and, sharply looking out,
Soon may'st thou find a mistress in the rout,
For length of time, or for a single bout.
The theatres are berries for the fair:
Like ants on mole-hills thither they repair;
Like bees to hives, so numerously they throng,
It may be said, they to that place belong.
Thither they swarm who have the public voice;
There choose, if plenty not distracts thy choice.
To see, and to be seen, in heaps they run;
Some to undo, and some to be undone.
  From Romulus the rise of plays began,
To his new subjects a commodious man;
Who, his unmarried soldiers to supply,
Took care the commonwealth should multiply,
Providing Sabine women for his braves,
Like a true king, to get a race of slaves.
His playhouse not of Parian marble made,
Nor was it spread with purple sails for shade;
The stage with rushes or with leaves they strowed,
No scenes in prospect, no machining god.
On rows of homely turf they sat to see,
Crowned with the wreaths of every common tree.
There, while they sit in rustic majesty,
Each lover had his mistress in his eye,

And whom he saw most suiting to his mind,
For joys of matrimonial rape designed.
Scarce could they wait the plaudit in their haste,
But, ere the dances and the song were past,
The monarch gave the signal from his throne,
And, rising, bade his merry men fall on.
The martial crew, like soldiers ready pressed,
Just at the word – the word too was 'the best' –
With joyful cries each other animate;
Some choose, and some at hazard seize their mate.
As doves from eagles, or from wolves the lambs,
So from their lawless lovers fly the dames.
Their fear was one, but not one face of fear;
Some rend the lovely tresses of their hair,
Some shriek, and some are struck with dumb despair.
Her absent mother one invokes in vain,
One stands amazed, not daring to complain;
The nimbler trust their feet, the slow remain.
But nought availing, all are captives led,
Trembling and blushing, to the genial bed.
She who too long resisted, or denied,
The lusty lover made by force a bride,
And with superior strength compelled her to his side.
Then soothed her thus: 'My soul's far better part,
Cease weeping, nor afflict thy tender heart;
For what thy father to thy mother was,
That faith to thee, that solemn vow I pass.'
   Thus Romulus became so popular:
This was the way to thrive in peace and war;
To pay his army, and fresh whores to bring:
Who would not fight for such a gracious king?
Thus love in theatres did first improve,
And theatres are still the scene of love.
Nor shun the chariot's, and the courser's race;

The circus is no inconvenient place.
No need is there of talking on the hand;
Nor nods, nor signs, which lovers understand:
But boldly next the fair your seat provide;
Close as you can to hers, and side by side.
Pleased or unpleased, no matter, crowding sit:
For so the laws of public shows permit.
Then find occasion to begin discourse;
Enquire whose chariot this, and whose that horse.
To whatsoever side she is inclined,
Suit all your inclinations to her mind;
Like what she likes; from thence your court begin;
And whom she favours, wish that he may win.
But when the statues of the deities,
In chariots rolled, appear before the prize;
When Venus comes, with deep devotion rise.
If dust be on her lap, or grains of sand,
Brush both away with your officious hand;
If none be there, yet brush that nothing thence,
And still to touch her lap make some pretence.
Touch anything of hers; and if her train
Sweep on the ground, let it not sweep in vain,
But gently take it up, and wipe it clean;
And while you wipe it, with observing eyes,
Who knows but you may see her naked thighs!
Observe who sits behind her; and beware,
Lest his encroaching knee should press the fair.
Light service takes light minds, for some can tell
Of favours won, by laying cushions well.
By fanning faces, some their fortune meet;
And some by laying footstools for their feet.
These overtures of love the circus gives;
Nor at the sword-play less the lover thrives;
For there the son of Venus fights his prize,

And deepest wounds are oft received from eyes.
One, while the crowd their acclamations make,
Or while he bets, and puts his ring to stake,
Is struck from far, and feels the flying dart,
And of the spectacle is made a part.

### (2)

*The hazards of one's mistress' birthday.*

But than her birthday seldom comes a worse,
When bribes and presents must be sent of course;
And that's a bloody day, that costs thy purse.
Be staunch, yet parsimony will be vain;
The craving sex will still the lover drain.
No skill can shift 'em off, nor art remove;
They will be begging when they know we love.
The merchant comes upon th' appointed day,
Who shall before thy face his wares display;
To choose for her she craves thy kind advice,
Then begs again, to bargain for the price;
But when she has her purchase in her eye,
She hugs thee close, and kisses thee to buy:
"Tis what I want, and 'tis a penn'orth too;
In many years I will not trouble you!'
If you complain you have no ready coin;
No matter, 'tis but writing of a line:
A little bill, not to be paid at sight;
Now curse the time when thou wert taught to write!
She keeps her birthday; you must send the cheer,
And she'll be born a hundred times a year.
With daily lies she dribs thee into cost;
That earring dropped a stone, that ring is lost.
They often borrow what they never pay:
Whate'er you lend her, think it thrown away.

Had I ten mouths and tongues to tell each art,
All would be wearied ere I told a part.

### (3)

*Wine and love: the story of Bacchus and Ariadne.*

Now Bacchus calls me to his jolly rites;
Who would not follow, when a god invites?
He helps the poet, and his pen inspires:
Kind and indulgent to his former fires.
  Fair Ariadne wandered on the shore,
Forsaken now, and Theseus loves no more:
Loose was her gown, dishevelled was her hair,
Her bosom naked, and her feet were bare;
Exclaiming, in the water's brink she stood;
Her briny tears augment the briny flood.
She shrieked, and wept, and both became her face;
No posture could that heavenly form disgrace.
She beat her breast: 'The traitor's gone,' said she,
'What shall become of poor forsaken me?
What shall become' – she had not time for more;
The sounding cymbals rattled on the shore;
She swoons for fear, she falls upon the ground;
No vital heat was in her body found.
The Mimallonian dames about her stood,
And scudding satyrs ran before their god.
Silenus on his ass did next appear,
And held upon the mane (the god was clear).
The drunken sire pursues, the dames retire;
Sometimes the drunken dames pursue the drunken sire.
At last he topples over on the plain;
The satyrs laugh, and bid him rise again.
And now the god of wine came driving on,
High on his chariot, by swift tigers drawn.

Her colour, voice and sense forsook the fair;
Thrice did her trembling feet for flight prepare,
And thrice, affrighted, did her flight forbear.
She shook, like leaves of corn when tempests blow,
Or slender reeds that in the marshes grow.
To whom the god: 'Compose thy fearful mind;
In me a truer husband thou shalt find.
With heaven I will endow thee, and thy star
Shall with propitious light be seen afar,
And guide on seas the doubtful mariner.'
  He said, and from his chariot leaping light,
Lest the grim tigers should the nymph affright,
His brawny arms around her waist he threw –
For gods, whate'er they will with ease can do –
And swiftly bore her thence: th' attending throng
Shout at the sight, and sing the nuptial song.
Now in full bowls her sorrow she may steep;
The bridegroom's liquor lays the bride asleep.

(trans. John Dryden)

# from Fasti ('Calendar')

## from Book 2: February

### (1)

*The origins of the 'Dolphin' constellation.*

The Dolphin, whom you lately saw so bright,
Will wholly be obscured the following night;
Whether as for a happy spy to love
He gained a place among the stars above;
Or whether for Arion, whom he bore
Upon his back, and carried safe to shore;
  Who has not heard of sweet Arion's fame?
What country is a stranger to his name?
He that, with music's all-enchanting force,
Could stop a running river in its course;
Whose voice with magic virtue was endued,
To stop a wolf, though he his prey pursued;
The dog and hare their fleeting course have stayed,
To listen when upon his lyre he played;
A furious bull his music could assuage,
And mollify the furious lion's rage;
The crow and owl, the hawk and dove, were friends,
To sit and hear his soft melodious strains;
And Cynthia in her orb reluctant hung,
As if she heard her brother's tuneful song.
Long had he ravished the Sicilian plains,
And charmed Ausonia with his lyric strains;
From thence returning home he went aboard,
And in the ship his late-got riches stored;
Perhaps, Arion, thou the sea might'st fear;
Trust not the ship, there is no safety there!
The master and the crew, with sword in hand,

Seize on the lyrist, and his wealth demand;
'But why these hostile arms?' Arion cried,
'Stick to your tackling, and the vessel guide;
Free from all guilt, I'm not afraid to die,
But let me first sing my own elegy.'

They grant him leave, but laugh at his request;
Then with a chaplet crowned, and richly dressed
In a wrought mantle, which they all admire,
He with his fingers touched the sounding lyre,
And, like the dying swan, he sweetly sung,
The sounding lyre according with his tongue;
This done, and thus adorned, without delay,
Springing he jumped into the foamy sea;
Where, wondrous to relate, a dolphin heaved
His bending back and kind the man received;
On whom he sat, and played with tuneful hand,
Till that the dolphin brought him safe to land.

To gracious heaven let innocency trust,
The gods reward the pious, and the just;
It was for this Jove made the dolphin shine,
A constellation; and his stars are nine.


### (2)

*Tarquin, King of Rome, is seized with lust for Lucretia, the virtuous wife of Collatinus. He returns to Rome from the siege of Ardea, intent on her seduction or rape.*

The day was spent, the sun was nearly set,
When he arrived before Collatia's gate.
Like as a friend, but with a sly intent,
To Collatinus' house he boldly went;
There he a kind reception met within
From fair Lucretia, for they were akin.
What ignorance attends the human mind!

How oft we are to our misfortunes blind!
Thoughtless of harm, she made a handsome feast,
And o'er a cheerful glass regaled her guest
With lively chat, and then to bed they went.
But Tarquin still pursued his vile intent;
All dark, about the dead of night he rose,
And softly to Lucretia's chamber goes;
His naked sword he carried in his hand,
That what he could not win, he might command;
With rapture on her bed himself he threw,
And as approaching to her lips he drew,
'Dear cousin, ah, my dearest life,' he said,
''Tis I, 'tis Tarquin, why are you afraid?'
Trembling with fear she not a word could say,
Her spirits fled, she fainted quite away;
Like as a lamb beneath a wolf's rude paws,
Appalled and stunned, her breath she hardly draws;
What can she do? Resistance would be vain:
She a weak woman, he a vigorous man.
Should she cry out? His naked sword was by,
'One scream,' said he, 'and you this instant die!'
Should she escape? His hands lay on her breast,
Now first by hands of any stranger pressed;
The lover urged by threats, rewards and prayers,
But neither prayers, rewards nor threats she hears;
'Will you not yield?' he cries. 'Then know my will,
When these my warm desires have had their fill;
By your dead corpse I'll kill and lay a slave,
And in that posture both together leave;
Then feign myself a witness of your shame,
And fix a lasting blemish on your fame.'
   Her mind the fears of blemished fame control,
And shake the resolutions of her soul;
'But of thy conquest, Tarquin, never boast,

Gaining that sort, thou hast a kingdom lost;
Vengeance thy complicated guilt attends,
Which both in thine, and family's ruin ends.'
   With rising day the sad Lucretia rose,
Her inward grief her outward habit shows;
Mournful she sat in tears, and all alone,
As if she'd lost her only darling son;
Then for her husband and her father sent,
Who Ardea left in haste, to know th' intent;
Who, when they saw her all in mourning dressed,
To know th' occasion of her grief request;
Whose funeral she mourned, desired to know,
Or why she had put on those robes of woe.
She long concealed the melancholy cause,
While from her eyes a briny fountain flows;
Her agèd sire and tender husband strive
To heal her grief, and words of comfort give;
Yet dread some fatal consequence to hear,
And begged she would the cruel cause declare;
Thrice she began the unexpected tale,
And thrice her feeble voice and spirits fail;
Her next attempt with downcast eyes she made,
'And must I utter my disgrace?' she said.
'Are these the conquests we to Tarquin owe?'
And all she could with modest language show,
She then related, while with weeping eyes
Her words create their anger and surprise.
But then from guilt, or any show of blame,
Her sire and husband both absolve the dame.
   'What you,' said she, 'forgive, I can't forgive;
Her honour lost, how can Lucretia live?'
Then straight the poniard hid beneath her vest
She boldly plunged into her snowy breast;
Before her father's feet she tumbled down,

Adjusting as she fell her flowing gown:
This was her last, this was her dying care,
That she might then with decency appear.
                              (trans. William Massey)

# from Metamorphoses ('Transformations')

## from Book 1

### (1)

*The creation of the earth out of chaos.*

Of bodies changed to various forms I sing:
Ye gods, from whom these miracles did spring,
Inspire my numbers with celestial heat,
Till I my long laborious work complete,
And add perpetual tenor to my rhymes,
Deduced from Nature's birth to Caesar's times.
  Before the seas, and this terrestrial ball,
And heaven's high canopy, that covers all,
One was the face of Nature, if a face –
Rather a rude and indigested mass:
A lifeless lump, unfashioned and unframed,
Of jarring seeds, and justly Chaos named.
No sun was lighted up the world to view;
No moon did yet her blunted horns renew,
Nor yet was earth suspended in the sky,
Nor, poised, did on her own foundations lie,
Nor seas about the shores their arms had thrown;
But earth and air and water were in one.
Thus air was void of light, and earth unstable,
And water's dark abyss unnavigable.
No certain form on any was impressed;
All were confused, and each disturbed the rest.
For hot and cold were in one body fixed,
And soft with hard, and light with heavy mixed.
  But God or Nature, while they thus contend,
To these intestine discords put an end:
Then earth from air, and seas from earth were driven,

And grosser air sunk from ethereal heaven.
Thus disembroiled, they take their proper place;
The next of kin contiguously embrace,
And foes are sundered by a larger space.
The force of fire ascended first on high,
And took its dwelling in the vaulted sky;
Then air succeeds, in lightness next to fire,
Whose atoms from unactive earth retire.
Earth sinks beneath, and draws a numerous throng
Of ponderous, thick, unwieldy seeds along.
About her coasts unruly waters roar,
And, rising on a ridge, insult the shore.
  Thus when the god, whatever god was he,
Had formed the whole, and made the parts agree,
That no unequal portions might be found,
He moulded earth into a spacious round:
Then with a breath he gave the winds to blow,
And bade the congregated waters flow.
He adds the running springs, and standing lakes,
And bounding banks for winding rivers makes.
Some part in earth are swallowed up, the most
In ample oceans, disembogued, are lost.
He shades the woods, the valleys he restrains
With rocky mountains, and extends the plains.

## (2)

*The creation of Man*

A creature of a more exalted kind
Was wanting yet, and then was Man designed:
Conscious of thought, of more capacious breast,
For empire formed, and fit to rule the rest:
Whether with particles of heavenly fire
The god of nature did his soul inspire,

Or earth, but new divided from the sky,
And pliant still retained th' ethereal energy –
Which wise Prometheus tempered into paste,
And mixed with living streams, the godlike image cast.
Thus, while the mute creation downward bend
Their sight, and to their earthy mother tend,
Man looks aloft, and with erected eyes
Beholds his own hereditary skies.
From such rude principles our form began;
And earth was metamorphosed into man.

### (3)

*Mankind degenerates through four ages: Gold, Silver, Iron and Bronze. To convince his fellow-gods of mankind's corruption, Jupiter narrates his encounter with the tyrant, Lycaon.*

Disguised in human shape, I travelled round
The world, and more than what I heard, I found.
O'er Maenalus I took my steepy way,
By caverns infamous for beasts of prey;
Then crossed Cyllene, and the piny shade
More infamous by cursed Lycaon made.
Dark night had covered heaven and earth, before
I entered his unhospitable door.
Just at my entrance, I displayed the sign
That somewhat was approaching of divine.
The prostrate people pray; the tyrant grins;
And, adding profanation to his sins,
'I'll try,' said he, 'and if a god appear,
To prove his deity shall cost him dear.'
'Twas late; the graceless wretch my death prepares,
When I should soundly sleep, oppressed with cares.
  This dire experiment he chose, to prove
If I were mortal, or undoubted Jove:

But first he had resolved to taste my power.
Not long before, but in a luckless hour
Some legates, sent from the Molossian state,
Were on a peaceful errand come to treat.
Of these he murders one, he boils the flesh;
And lays the mangled morsels in a dish;
Some part he roasts, then serves it up, so dressed,
And bids me welcome to this human feast.
Moved with disdain, the table I o'erturned;
And with avenging flames the palace burned.
The tyrant in a fright for shelter gains
The neighbouring fields, and scours along the plains.
Howling he fled, and fain he would have spoke;
But human voice his brutal tongue forsook.
About his lips the gathered foam he churns,
And, breathing slaughters, still with rage he burns,
But on the bleating flock his fury turns.
His mantle, now his hide, with rugged hairs
Cleaves to his back; a famished face he bears;
His arms descend, his shoulders sink away
To multiply his legs for chase of prey.
He grows a wolf, his hoariness remains,
And the same rage in other members reigns.
His eyes still sparkle in a narrower space:
His jaws retain the grin and violence of his face.

### (4)

*Jupiter sends a flood to destroy the inhabitants of the earth.*

One climbs a cliff, one in his boat is borne,
And ploughs above, where late he sowed his corn.
Others o'er chimney-tops and turrets row,
And drop their anchors on the meads below:
Or, downward driv'n, they bruise the tender vine,

Or, tossed aloft, are knocked against a pine.
And where of late the kids had cropped the grass,
The monsters of the deep now take their place.
Insulting Nereids on the cities ride,
And wondering dolphins o'er the palace glide.
On leaves and masts of mighty oaks they browse;
And their broad fins entangle in the boughs.
The frighted wolf now swims amongst the sheep;
The yellow lion wanders in the deep;
His rapid force no longer helps the boar;
The stag swims faster than he ran before.
The fowls, long beating on their wings in vain,
Despair of land, and drop into the main.
Now hills and vales no more distinction know;
And levelled nature lies oppressed below.
The most of mortals perish in the flood;
The small remainder dies for want of food.

(5)

*Deucalion and Pyrrha, the sole human survivors of the flood,
are told by the goddess Themis to throw 'their mother's bones'
behind them. Deucalion surmises that this means the stones in
Mother Earth.*

Descending from the mount, they first unbind
Their vests and, veiled, they cast the stones behind:
The stones – a miracle to mortal view,
But long tradition makes it pass for true –
Did first the rigour of their kind expel,
And suppled into softness as they fell;
Then swelled, and swelling, by degrees grew warm;
And took the rudiments of human form.
Imperfect shapes: in marble such are seen,
When the rude chisel does the man begin;

While yet the roughness of the stone remains,
Without the rising muscles and the veins.
The sappy parts, and next resembling juice,
Were turned to moisture, for the bodies' use:
Supplying humours, blood and nourishment;
The rest, too solid to receive a bent,
Converts to bones; and what was once a vein,
Its former name and nature did retain.
By help of power divine, in little space,
What the man threw assumed a manly face;
And what the wife renewed the female race.
Hence we derive our nature: born to bear
Laborious life, and hardened into care.

### (6)

*The god Apollo is smitten with love for the reluctant nymph, Daphne.*

The first and fairest of his loves was she
Whom not blind Fortune but the dire decree
Of angry Cupid forced him to desire:
Daphne her name, and Peneus was her sire.
Swelled with the pride that new success attends,
He sees the stripling, while his bow he bends,
And thus insults him. 'Thou lascivious boy,
Are arms like these for children to employ?
Know, such achievements are my proper claim,
Due to my vigour, and unerring aim:
Resistless are my shafts, and Python late
In such a feathered death has found his fate.
Take up thy torch, and lay my weapons by:
With that the feeble souls of lovers fry.'
  To whom the son of Venus thus replied:
'Phoebus, thy shafts are sure on all beside,
But mine on Phoebus, mine the fame shall be

But said her wish would prove her punishment:
For so much youth and so much beauty joined,
Opposed the state which her desires designed.
  The god of light, aspiring to her bed,
Hopes what he seeks, with flattering fancies fed,
And is by his own oracles misled.
And as in empty fields the stubble burns,
Or nightly travellers, when day returns,
Their useless torches on dry hedges throw,
That catch the flames and kindle all the row;
So burns the god, consuming in desire,
And feeding in his breast a fruitless fire:
Her well-turned neck he viewed (her neck was bare)
And on her shoulders her dishevelled hair;
'Oh were it combed,' said he, 'with what a grace
Would every waving curl become her face!'
He viewed her eyes, like heavenly lamps that shone,
He viewed her lips, too sweet to view alone,
Her taper fingers, and her panting breast;
He praises all he sees, and for the rest
Believes the beauties yet unseen are best.
Swift as the wind the damsel fled away,
Nor did for these alluring speeches stay:
  'Stay nymph,' he cried, 'I follow, not a foe.
Thus from the lion trips the trembling doe;
Thus from the wolf the frightened lamb removes,
And, from pursuing falcons, fearful doves;
Thou shunn'st a god, and shunn'st a god that loves.
Ah, lest some thorn should pierce thy tender foot,
Or thou shouldst fall in flying my pursuit!
To sharp uneven ways thy steps decline:
Abate thy speed, and I will bate of mine!
Yet think from whom thou dost so rashly fly;
Nor basely born, nor shepherd's swain am I.

Perhaps thou know'st not my superior state,
And from that ignorance proceeds thy hate.
Me Claros, Delphos, Tenedos obey;
These hands the Patareian sceptre sway.
The king of gods begot me: what shall be,
Or is, or ever was, in fate I see.
Mine is th' invention of the charming lyre;
Sweet notes and heavenly numbers I inspire.
Sure is my bow, unerring is my dart;
But ah, more deadly his who pierced my heart!
Med'cine is mine; what herbs and simples grow
In fields and forests, all their powers I know,
And am the great physician called below.'

  Alas, that fields and forests can afford
No remedies to heal their lovesick lord!
To cure the pains of love no plant avails:
And his own physic the physician fails.

  She heard not half, so furiously she flies,
And on her ear th' imperfect accent dies.
Fear gave her wings, and as she fled the wind,
Increasing, spread her flowing hair behind,
And left her legs and thighs exposed to view –
Which made the god more eager to pursue.
The god was young, and was too hotly bent
To lose his time in empty compliment;
But led by love, and fired with such a sight,
Impetuously pursued his near delight.

  As when th' impatient greyhound, slipped from far,
Bounds o'er the glebe to course the fearful hare;
She in her speed does all her safety lay,
And he with double speed pursues the prey;
O'er-runs her at the sitting turn, and licks
His chaps in vain, and blows upon the flix:
She 'scapes, and for the neighbouring covert strives,

And gaining shelter, doubts if yet she lives:
If little things with great we may compare,
Such was the god, and such the flying fair.
She, urged by fear, her feet did swiftly move;
But he more swiftly who was urged by love.
He gathers ground upon her in the chase,
Now breathes upon her hair with nearer pace,
And just is fastening on the wished embrace.
  The nymph grew pale, and in a mortal fright,
Spent with the labour of so long a flight;
And now despairing, cast a mournful look
Upon the streams of her paternal brook:
'Oh help,' she cried, 'in this extremest need,
If water gods are deities indeed:
Gape earth, and this unhappy wretch entomb;
Or change my form, whence all my sorrows come!'
  Scarce had she finished, when her feet she found
Benumbed with cold, and fastened to the ground:
A filmy rind about her body grows;
Her hair to leaves, her arms extend to boughs:
The nymph is all into a laurel gone:
The smoothness of her skin remains alone.
Yet Phoebus loves her still, and casting round
Her bole his arms, some little warmth he found.
The tree still panted in th' unfinished part:
Not wholly vegetive, and heaved her heart.
He fixed his lips upon the trembling rind;
It swerved aside, and his embrace declined;
To whom the god: 'Because thou canst not be
My mistress, I espouse thee for my tree:
Be thou the prize of honour and renown;
The deathless poet, and the poem crown.
Thou shalt the Roman festivals adorn,
And, after poets, be by victors worn.

Thou shalt returning Caesar's triumph grace;
When pomps shall in a long procession pass,
Wreathed on the posts before his palace wait;
And be the sacred guardian of the gate.
Secure from thunder, and unharmed by Jove,
Unfading as th' immortal powers above:
And as the locks of Phoebus are unshorn,
So shall perpetual green thy boughs adorn.'
  The grateful tree was pleased with what he said;
And shook the shady honours of her head.

(trans. John Dryden)

## from Book 2

   (1)

*Apollo ill-advisedly allows his son Phaethon to drive the chariot of the sun. Despite his father's warnings, the youth soon finds himself out of control.*

Half dead with sudden fear he dropped the reins;
The horses felt 'em loose upon their manes,
And, flying out through all the plains above,
Ran uncontrolled where'er their fury drove;
Rushed on the stars, and through a pathless way
Of unknown regions hurried on the day.
And now above, and now below they flew,
And near the earth the burning chariot drew.
  The clouds disperse in fumes, the wondering moon
Beholds her brother's steeds beneath her own;
The highlands smoke, cleft by the piercing rays,
Or, clad with woods, in their own fuel blaze.
Next o'er the plains, where ripened harvests grow,
The running conflagration spreads below . . .
  Th' astonished youth, where'er his eyes could turn,

Beheld the universe around him burn:
The world was in a blaze; nor could he bear
The sultry vapours and the scorching air,
Which from below, as from a furnace, flowed;
And now the axle-tree beneath him glowed:
Lost in the whirling clouds that round him broke,
And white with ashes, hovering in the smoke,
He flew where'er the horses drove, nor knew
Whither the horses drove, or where he flew.

  'Twas then, they say, the swarthy Moor begun
To change his hue, and blacken in the sun.
Then Libya first, of all her moisture drained,
Became a barren waste, a wild of sand.

### (2)

*The scorched Earth asks for help. Jupiter strikes Phaethon from his chariot.*

Jove called to witness every power above,
And ev'n the god whose son the chariot drove,
That what he acts he is compelled to do,
Or universal ruin must ensue.
Straight he ascends the high ethereal throne,
From whence he used to dart his thunder down,
From whence his showers and storms he used to pour,
But now could meet with neither storm nor shower.
Then, aiming at the youth, with lifted hand,
Full at his head he hurled the forky brand,
In dreadful thunderings. Thus th' almighty sire
Suppressed the raging of the fires with fire.

  At once from life, and from the chariot driven,
Th' ambitious boy fell thunder-struck from heaven.
The horses started with a sudden bound,
And flung the reins and chariot to the ground:

The studded harness from their necks they broke;
Here fell a wheel, and here a silver spoke,
Here were the beam and axle torn away;
And scattered o'er the earth the shining fragments lay.
The breathless Phaethon, with flaming hair,
Shot from the chariot like a falling star,
That in a summer's evening from the top
Of heaven drops down, or seems at least to drop;
Till on the Po his blasted corpse was hurled,
Far from his country, in the western world.

### (3)

*Jupiter seduces Europa, the daughter of Agenor, King of Sidon, in the guise of a bull.*

The dignity of empire laid aside,
(For love but ill agrees with kingly pride)
The ruler of the skies, the thundering god,
Who shakes the world's foundations with a nod,
Among a herd of lowing heifers ran,
Frisked in a bull, and bellowed o'er the plain.
Large rolls of fat about his shoulders clung,
And from his neck the double dewlap hung.
His skin was whiter than the snow that lies
Unsullied by the breath of southern skies;
Small shining horns on his curled forehead stand,
As turned and polished by the workman's hand;
His eyeballs rolled, not formidably bright,
But gazed and languished with a gentle light.
His ev'ry look was peaceful, and expressed
The softness of the lover in the beast.
    Agenor's royal daughter, as she played
Among the fields, the milk-white bull surveyed,
And viewed his spotless body with delight,

And at a distance kept him in her sight.
At length she plucked the rising flowers, and fed
The gentle beast, and fondly stroked his head.
He stood, well-pleased to touch the charming fair,
But hardly could confine his pleasure there.
And now he wantons o'er the neighbouring strand,
Now rolls his body on the yellow sand;
And, now perceiving all her fears decayed,
Comes tossing forward to the royal maid;
Gives her his breast to stroke, and downward turns
His grisly brow, and gentle stoops his horns.
In flowery wreaths the royal virgin dressed
His bending horns, and kindly clapped his breast.
Till now grown wanton, and devoid of fear,
Not knowing that she pressed the Thunderer,
She placed herself upon his back, and rode
O'er fields and meadows, seated on the god.
  He gently marched along, and by degrees
Left the dry meadow, and approached the seas;
Where now he dips his hoofs and wets his thighs,
Now plunges in, and carries off the prize.
The frighted nymph looks backward on the shore,
And hears the tumbling billows round her roar;
But still she holds him fast: one hand is borne
Upon his back, the other grasps a horn;
Her train of ruffling garments flies behind,
Swells in the air, and hovers in the wind.

# from Book 3

## (1)

*The story of Europa concluded.*

Through storms and tempests he the virgin bore,
And lands her safe on the Dictean shore;
Where now, in his divinest form arrayed,
In his true shape he captivates the maid;
Who gazes on him, and with wondering eyes
Beholds the new majestic figure rise,
His glowing features, and celestial light,
And all the god discovered to her sight.

## (2)

*The huntsman Actaeon strays into a grotto which is used by the goddess Diana as her private retreat.*

Down in a vale with pine and cypress clad,
Refreshed with gentle winds, and brown with shade,
The chaste Diana's private haunt, there stood
Full in the centre of the darksome wood
A spacious grotto, all around o'ergrown
With hoary moss, and arched with pumice-stone.
From out its rocky clefts the waters flow,
And trickling swell into a lake below.
Nature had everywhere so played her part,
That everywhere she seemed to vie with art.
Here the bright goddess, toiled and chafed with heat,
Was wont to bathe her in the cool retreat.
  Here did she now with all her train resort,
Panting with heat, and breathless from the sport;
Her armour-bearer laid her bow aside,
Some loosed her sandals, some her veil untied;
Each busy nymph her proper part undressed;

While Crocale, more handy than the rest,
Gathered her flowing hair, and in a noose
Bound it together, whilst her own hung loose.
Five of the more ignoble sort by turns
Fetch up the water, and unlade their urns.
  Now all undressed the shining goddess stood,
When young Actaeon, wildered in the wood,
To the cool grot by his hard fate betrayed,
The fountains filled with naked nymphs surveyed.
The frighted virgins shrieked at the surprise;
The forest echoed with their piercing cries.
Then in a huddle round their goddess pressed:
She, proudly eminent above the rest,
With blushes glowed: such blushes as adorn
The ruddy welkin, or the purple morn;
And though the crowding nymphs her body hide,
Half backward shrunk, and viewed him from aside.
Surprised, at first she would have snatched her bow,
But sees the circling waters round her flow;
These in the hollow of her hand she took,
And dashed 'em in his face, while thus she spoke:
'Tell if thou can'st the wondrous sight disclosed,
A goddess naked to thy view exposed.'
  This said, the man begun to disappear
By slow degrees, and ended in a deer.
A rising horn on either brow he wears,
And stretches out his neck, and pricks his ears;
Rough is his skin, with sudden hairs o'ergrown,
His bosom pants with fears before unknown.
Transformed at length, he flies away in haste,
And wonders why he flies away so fast.
But as by chance, within a neighbouring brook,
He saw his branching horns and altered look;
Wretched Actaeon, in a doleful tone

He tried to speak, but only gave a groan!
And as he wept, within the watery glass
He saw the big round drops, with silent pace,
Run trickling down a savage hairy face.
What should he do? Or seek his old abodes,
Or herd among the deer, and skulk in woods?
Here shame dissuades him, there his fear prevails,
And each by turns his aching heart assails.
  As he thus ponders, he behind him spies
His opening hounds, and now he hears their cries:
A generous pack, or to maintain the chase,
Or snuff the vapour from the scented grass.
He bounded off with fear, and swiftly ran
O'er craggy mountains, and the flowery plain;
Through brakes and thickets forced his way, and flew
Through many a ring, where once he did pursue.
In vain he oft endeavoured to proclaim
His new misfortune, and to tell his name;
Nor voice nor words the brutal tongue supplies;
From shouting men, and horns, and dogs he flies,
Deafened and stunned with their promiscuous cries.
When now the fleetest of the pack, that pressed
Close at his heels, and sprung before the rest,
Had fastened on him, straight another pair
Hung on his wounded haunch, and held him there,
Till all the pack came up, and every hound
Tore the sad huntsman grovelling on the ground,
Who now appeared but one continued wound.
With dropping tears his bitter fate he moans,
And fills the mountain with his dying groans.
His servants with a piteous look he spies,
And turns about his supplicating eyes.
His servants, ignorant of what had chanced,
With eager haste and joyful shouts advanced,

And called their lord Actaeon to the game:
He shook his head in answer to the name;
He heard, but wished he had indeed been gone,
Or only to have stood a looker-on.
But to his grief he finds himself too near,
And feels his ravenous dogs with fury tear
Their wretched master panting in a deer.

### (3)

*Narcissus, a proud youth, is loved by the nymph Echo.*

Narcissus now his sixteenth year began,
Just turned of boy, and on the verge of man;
Many a friend the blooming youth caressed,
Many a lovesick maid her flame confessed:
Such was his pride, in vain the friend caressed,
The lovesick maid in vain her flame confessed.
  Once, in the woods, as he pursued the chase,
The babbling Echo had descried his face;
She, who in others' words her silence breaks,
Nor speaks herself but when another speaks.
Echo was then a maid, of speech bereft,
Of wonted speech; for though her voice was left,
Juno a curse did on her tongue impose,
To sport with every sentence in the close.
Full often when the goddess might have caught
Jove and her rivals in the very fault,
This nymph with subtle stories would delay
Her coming till the lovers slipped away.
The goddess found out the deceit in time,
And then she cried, 'That tongue, for this thy crime,
Which could so many subtle tales produce,
Shall be hereafter but of little use!'
Hence 'tis she prattles in a fainter tone,

With mimic sounds, and accents not her own.
   This lovesick virgin, overjoyed to find
The boy alone, still followed him behind;
When glowing warmly at her near approach,
As sulphur blazes at the taper's touch,
She longed her hidden passion to reveal,
And tell her pains, but had not words to tell:
She can't begin, but waits for the rebound,
To catch his voice, and to return the sound.
   The nymph, when nothing could Narcissus move,
Still dashed with blushes for her slighted love,
Lived in the shady covert of the woods,
In solitary caves and dark abodes;
Where pining wandered the rejected fair,
Till harassed out, and worn away with care,
The sounding skeleton, of blood bereft,
Besides her bones and voice had nothing left.
Her bones are petrified, her voice is found
In vaults, where still it doubles every sound.

## (4)

*Narcissus, bending over a fountain to drink, sees a beautiful face in the pool and falls in love with it, slowly coming to realize that it is his own reflection. He laments his plight.*

'You trees,' says he, 'and thou surrounding grove,
Who oft have been the kindly scenes of love,
Tell me, if e'er within your shades did lie
A youth so tortured, so perplexed as I?
I, who before me see the charming fair,
Whilst there he stands, and yet he stands not there:
In such a maze of love my thoughts are lost;
And yet no bulwarked town, nor distant coast,
Preserves the beauteous youth from being seen,

No mountains rise, nor oceans flow between.
A shallow water hinders my embrace;
And yet the lovely mimic wears a face
That kindly smiles, and when I bend to join
My lips to his, he fondly bends to mine.
Hear, gentle youth, and pity my complaint,
Come from thy well, thou fair inhabitant.
My charms an easy conquest have obtained
O'er other hearts, by thee alone disdained.
But why should I despair? I'm sure he burns
With equal flames, and languishes by turns.
Whene'er I stoop, he offers at a kiss,
And when my arms I stretch, he stretches his.
His eye with pleasure on my face he keeps,
He smiles my smiles, and when I weep he weeps.
Whene'er I speak, his moving lips appear
To utter something, which I cannot hear.

  Ah wretched me! I now begin too late
To find out all the long-perplexed deceit;
It is myself I love, myself I see;
The gay delusion is a part of me.
I kindle up the fires by which I burn,
And my own beauties from the well return.
Whom should I court? How utter my complaint?
Enjoyment but produces my restraint,
And too much plenty makes me die for want.
How gladly would I from myself remove,
And at a distance set the thing I love!
My breast is warmed with such unusual fire,
I wish him absent whom I most desire.
And now I faint with grief; my fate draws nigh;
In all the pride of blooming youth I die!
Death will the sorrows of my heart relieve.
Oh might the visionary youth survive,

I should with joy my latest breath resign!
But oh, I see his fate involved in mine.'

(5)

*As Narcissus weeps into the pool, the reflection fades, causing him to languish further. His distress is witnessed by Echo.*

She saw him in his present misery,
Whom, spite of all her wrongs, she grieved to see.
She answered sadly to the lover's moan,
Sighed back his sighs, and groaned to every groan:
'Ah youth, beloved in vain!' Narcissus cries;
'Ah youth, beloved in vain!' the nymph replies.
'Farewell', says he; the parting sound scarce fell
From his faint lips, but she replied, 'Farewell.'
Then on th' unwholesome earth he gasping lies,
Till death shuts up those self-admiring eyes.
To the cold shades his flitting ghost retires,
And in the Stygian waves itself admires.
  For him the Naiads and the Dryads mourn,
Whom the sad Echo answers in her turn;
And now the sister-nymphs prepare his urn:
When, looking for his corpse, they only found
A rising stalk, with yellow blossoms crowned.

(trans. Joseph Addison)

# from Book 4

## (1)

*The daughters of Mineus, refusing to take part in the rites of Bacchus,*
*pass the time by telling stories. They narrate the tale of Pyramus and*
*Thisbe, two lovers kept apart by their parents. Through a chink in the*
*wall that divides their houses, Pyramus and Thisbe agree to meet outside*
*the town at Ninus' tomb, where a mulberry tree grows.*

The loving Thisbe ev'n prevents the hour;
With cautious silence she unlocks the door,
And veils her face, and marching through the gloom
Swiftly arrives at th' assignation tomb.
For still the fearful sex can fearless prove;
Boldly they act, if spirited by love.
When lo! a lioness rushed o'er the plain,
Grimly besmeared with blood of oxen slain;
And what to the dire sight new horrors brought,
To slake her thirst the neighbouring spring she sought.
Which by the moon when trembling Thisbe spies,
Winged with her fear, swift as the wind she flies;
And in a cave recovers from her fright,
But dropped her veil, confounded in her flight.
When sated with repeated draughts, again
The queen of beasts scoured back along the plain,
She found the veil, and mouthing it all o'er,
With bloody jaws the lifeless prey she tore.
  The youth, who could not cheat his guards so soon,
Late came, and noted by the glimmering moon
Some savage feet, new printed on the ground,
His cheeks turned pale, his limbs no vigour found:
But when, advancing, on the veil he spied
Distained with blood, and ghastly torn, he cried,
'One night shall death to two young lovers give,

But she deserved unnumbered years to live!
'Tis I am guilty, I have thee betrayed,
Who came not early, as my charming maid.
Whatever slew thee, I the cause remain;
I named and fixed the place where thou wast slain.
Ye lions from your neighbouring dens repair,
Pity the wretch, this impious body tear!
But cowards thus for death can idly cry;
The brave still have it in their power to die.'
  Then to th' appointed tree he hastes away,
The veil first gathered, though all rent it lay:
The veil all rent, yet still itself endears,
He kissed and, kissing, washed it with his tears.
'Though rich,' he cried, 'with many a precious stain,
Still from my blood a deeper tincture gain!'
Then in his breast his shining sword he drowned,
And fell supine, extended on the ground.
As out again the blade he, dying, drew,
Out spun the blood, and streaming upwards flew.
So if a conduit-pipe e'er burst you saw,
Swift spring the gushing waters through the flaw:
Then spouting in a bow, they rise on high,
And a new fountain plays amid the sky.
The berries, stained with blood, began to show
A dark complexion, and forgot their snow;
While, fattened with the flowing gore, the root
Was doomed for ever to a purple fruit.


### (2)

*Thisbe returns, and finds Pyramus dying.*

'And is it thus, ah, thus we meet?' she cried.
'My Pyramus, whence sprung thy cruel fate?
My Pyramus – ah, speak, ere 'tis too late!

I, thy own Thisbe, but one word implore,
One word thy Thisbe never asked before.'
At Thisbe's name, awaked, he opened wide
His dying eyes; with dying eyes he tried
On her to dwell, but closed them slow, and died.

  The fatal cause was now at last explored,
Her veil she knew, and saw his sheathless sword.
'From thy own hand thy ruin thou hast found,'
She said, 'but love first taught that hand to wound.
Ev'n I for thee as bold a hand can show,
And love, which shall as true direct the blow.
I will against the woman's weakness strive,
And never thee, lamented youth, survive.
The world may say I caused, alas, thy death,
But saw thee breathless, and resigned my breath.
Fate, though it conquers, shall no triumph gain;
Fate, that divides us, still divides in vain.
Now, both our cruel parents, hear my prayer,
My prayer to offer for us both I dare:
Oh, see our ashes in one urn confined,
Whom love at first, and fate at last has joined.
The bliss you envied is not our request;
Lovers, when dead, may sure together rest.
Thou, tree, where now one lifeless lump is laid,
Ere long o'er two shalt cast a friendly shade.
Still let our loves from thee be understood,
Still witness in thy purple fruit our blood.'

  She spoke, and in her bosom plunged the sword,
All warm and reeking from its slaughtered lord.
The prayer which dying Thisbe had preferred,
Both gods and parents with compassion heard.
The whiteness of the mulberry soon fled,
And ripening, saddened in a dusky red:

While both their parents their lost children mourn,
And mix their ashes in one golden urn.

### (3)

*The bashful Hermaphroditus rejects the Naiad Salmacis. She pretends to leave him, but watches him unseen as he bathes.*

The boy now fancies all the danger o'er,
And innocently sports about the shore,
Playful and wanton to the stream he trips,
And dips his foot, and shivers as he dips.
The coolness pleased him, and with eager haste
His airy garments on the banks he cast;
His godlike features, and his heavenly hue,
And all his beauties were exposed to view.
His naked limbs the nymph with rapture spies,
While hotter passions in her bosom rise,
Flush in her cheeks, and sparkle in her eyes.
She longs, she burns to clasp him in her arms,
And looks, and sighs, and kindles at his charms.
  Now all undressed upon the banks he stood,
And clasped his sides, and leaped into the flood:
His lovely limbs the silver waves divide,
His limbs appear more lovely through the tide,
As lilies shut within a crystal case
Receive a glossy lustre from the glass.
'He's mine, he's all my own!' the Naiad cries,
And flings off all, and after him she flies.
And now she fastens on him as he swims,
And holds him close, and wraps about his limbs.
The more the boy resisted, and was coy,
The more she clipped, and kissed the struggling boy.
So when the wriggling snake is snatched on high
In eagle's claws, and hisses in the sky,

Around the foe his twirling tail he flings,
And twists her legs, and writhes about her wings.
  The restless boy still obstinately strove
To free himself, and still refused her love.
Amidst his limbs she kept her limbs entwined,
'And why, coy youth,' she cries, 'why thus unkind?
Oh may the gods thus keep us ever joined!
Oh may we never, never part again!'
So prayed the nymph, nor did she pray in vain:
For now she finds him, as his limbs she pressed,
Grow nearer still, and nearer to her breast;
Till, piercing each the other's flesh, they run
Together, and incorporate in one:
Last in one face are both their faces joined,
As when the stock and grafted twig combined
Shoot up the same, and wear a common rind:
Both bodies in a single body mix,
A single body with a double sex.

                              (trans. Laurence Eusden)


## from Book 6

   (1)

*Arachne, despite being warned of her presumption, persists in challenging
Athene to a weaving contest.*

Straight to their posts appointed both repair,
And fix their threaded looms with equal care:
Around the solid beam the web is tied,
While hollow canes the parting warp divide;
Through which with nimble flight the shuttles play,
And for the woof prepare a ready way;
The woof and warp unite, pressed by the toothy slay.
  Thus both, their mantles buttoned to their breast,

Their skilful fingers ply with willing haste,
And work with pleasure; while they cheer the eye
With glowing purple of the Tyrian dye:
Or, justly intermixing shades with light,
Their colourings insensibly unite.
As when a shower, transpierced with sunny rays,
Its mighty arch along the heaven displays;
From whence a thousand different colours rise,
Whose fine transition cheats the clearest eyes;
So like the intermingled shading seems,
And only differs in the last extremes.
Then threads of gold both artfully dispose,
And, as each part in just proportion rose,
Some antique fable in their work disclose.

  Pallas in figures wrought the heavenly powers,
And Mars's hill among th' Athenian towers.
On lofty thrones twice six celestials sat,
Jove in the midst, and held their warm debate;
The subject weighty, and well known to fame,
From whom the city should receive its name.
Each god by proper features was expressed,
Jove with majestic mien excelled the rest.
His three-forked mace the dewy sea god shook,
And, looking sternly, smote the ragged rock;
When from the stone leaped forth a sprightly steed,
And Neptune claims the city for the deed.

  Herself she blazons with a glittering spear,
And crested helm that veiled her braided hair,
With shield, and scaly breastplate, implements of war.
Struck with her pointed lance, the teeming earth
Seemed to produce a new surprising birth;
When, from the glebe, the pledge of conquest sprung,
A tree pale-green with fairest olives hung.

## (2)

*In the corners of her tapestry, Athene weaves depictions of mortals who presumptuously dared to vie with the gods. Arachne, in her turn, depicts the love-intrigues of the Olympians.*

Arachne drew the famed intrigues of Jove,
Changed to a bull to gratify his love;
How through the briny tide all foaming hoar,
Lovely Europa on his back he bore.
The sea seemed waving, and the trembling maid
Shrunk up her tender feet, as if afraid;
And, looking back on the forsaken strand,
To her companions wafts her distant hand.
Next she designed Asteria's fabled rape,
When Jove assumed a soaring eagle's shape:
And showed how Leda lay supinely pressed,
Whilst the soft snowy swan sat hovering o'er her
   breast.
How in a satyr's form the god beguiled,
When fair Antiope with twins he filled.
Then, like Amphitryon, but a real Jove,
In fair Alcmena's arms he cooled his love.
In fluid gold to Danaë's heart he came,
Aegina felt him in a lambent flame.
He took Mnemosyne in shepherd's make,
And for Deois was a speckled snake.
  She made thee, Neptune, like a wanton steer,
Pacing the meads for love of Arnè dear;
Next like a stream, thy burning flame to slake,
And like a ram, for fair Bisaltis' sake.
Then Ceres in a steed your vigour tried,
Nor could the mare the yellow goddess hide.
Next to a fowl transformed, you won by force
The snake-haired mother of the wingèd horse;

And, in a dolphin's fishy form, subdued
Melantho sweet beneath the oozy flood.
 All these the maid with lively features drew,
And opened proper landscapes to the view.
There Phoebus, roving like a country swain,
Attunes his jolly pipe along the plain;
For lovely Isse's sake in shepherd's weeds,
O'er pastures green his bleating flock he feeds.
There Bacchus, imaged like the clustering grape,
Melting bedrops Erigone's fair lap;
And there old Saturn, stung with youthful heat,
Formed like a stallion, rushes to the feat.
Fresh flowers, which twists of ivy intertwine,
Mingling a running foliage, close the neat design.
 This the bright goddess, passionately moved,
With envy saw, yet inwardly approved.
The scene of heavenly guilt with haste she tore,
Nor longer the affront with patience bore;
A boxen shuttle in her hand she took,
And more than once Arachne's forehead struck.
Th' unhappy maid, impatient of the wrong,
Down from a beam her injured person hung;
When Pallas, pitying her wretched state,
At once prevented, and pronounced her fate;
'Live, but depend, vile wretch,' the goddess cried,
'Doomed in suspense for ever to be tied;
That all your race, to utmost date of time,
May feel the vengeance, and detest the crime.'
 Then, going off, she sprinkled her with juice,
Which leaves of baleful aconite produce.
Touched with the poisonous drug, her flowing hair
Fell to the ground, and left her temples bare;
Her usual features vanished from their place,
Her body lessened all, but most her face.

Her slender fingers, hanging on each side
With many joints, the use of legs supplied:
A spider's bag the rest, from which she gives
A thread, and still by constant weaving lives.

### (3)

*Tereus, King of Thrace, is smitten with an illicit passion for his
sister-in-law, Philomela. Having brought Philomela to visit his wife,
Procne, he savagely rapes her. She protests against her violation.*

'Savage, inhuman, cruel wretch!' she cries,
'Whom nor a parent's strict commands could move,
Though charged, and uttered with the tears of love;
Nor virgin innocence, nor all that's due
To the strong contract of the nuptial vow:
Virtue by this in wild confusion's laid,
And I compelled to wrong my sister's bed;
Whilst you, regardless of your marriage oath,
With stains of incest have defiled us both.
Though I deserved some punishment to find,
This was, ye gods, too cruel and unkind.
Yet, villain, to complete your horrid guilt,
Stab here, and let my tainted blood be spilt.
Oh happy, had it come before I knew
The cursed embrace of vile perfidious you!
Then my pale ghost, pure from incestuous love,
Had wandered spotless through th' Elysian grove.
But, if the gods above have power to know,
And judge those actions that are done below;
Unless the dreaded thunders of the sky,
Like me, subdued and violated lie;
Still my revenge shall take its proper time,
And suit the baseness of your hellish crime.
Myself, abandoned, and devoid of shame,

Through the wide world your actions will proclaim;
Or though I'm prisoned in this lonely den,
Obscured, and buried from the sight of men,
My mournful voice the pitying rocks shall move,
And my complainings echo through the grove.
Hear me, O heaven! And, if a god be there,
Let him regard me, and accept my prayer.'
  Struck with these words, the tyrant's guilty breast
With fear and anger was by turns possessed;
Now, with remorse his conscience deeply stung,
He drew the falchion that beside him hung,
And first her tender arms behind her bound,
Then dragged her by the hair along the ground.
The princess willingly her throat reclined,
And viewed the steel with a contented mind;
But soon her tongue the girding pinchers strain,
With anguish soon she feels the piercing pain:
'Oh father, father!' she would fain have spoke,
But the sharp torture her intention broke;
In vain she tries, for now the blade has cut
Her tongue sheer off, close to the trembling root.
The mangled part still quivered on the ground,
Murmuring with a faint imperfect sound:
And, as a serpent writhes his wounded train,
Uneasy, panting, and possessed with pain;
The piece, while life remained, still trembled fast,
And to its mistress pointed to the last.


### (4)

*The imprisoned Philomela weaves her story in a tapestry and sends it to Procne.*

What must unhappy Philomela do,
For ever subject to her keeper's view?

Huge walls of massy stone the lodge surround,
From her own mouth no way of speaking's found.
But all our wants by wit may be supplied,
And art makes up what fortune has denied:
With skill exact a Phrygian web she strung,
Fixed to a loom that in her chamber hung,
Where in-wrought letters, upon white displayed,
In purple notes her wretched case betrayed:
The piece, when finished, secretly she gave
Into the charge of one poor menial slave;
And then, with gestures, made him understand,
It must be safe conveyed to Procne's hand.
The slave with speed the queen's apartment sought,
And rendered up his charge, unknowing what he
  brought.
But when the cyphers, figured in each fold,
Her sister's melancholy story told,
(Strange that she could!) with silence she surveyed
The tragic piece, and without weeping read:
In such tumultuous haste her passions sprung,
They choked her voice, and quite disarmed her tongue.
No room for female tears; the Furies rise,
Darting vindictive glances from her eyes;
And, stung with rage, she bounds from place to place,
While stern revenge sits lowering in her face.


(5)

*Procne and Philomela resolve to take their revenge on Tereus by
killing his son, Itys, and cooking his flesh. Procne then invites
Tereus to a banquet.*

Asked by his wife to this inhuman feast,
Tereus unknowingly is made a guest:
Whilst she, her plot the better to disguise,

Styles it some unknown, mystic sacrifice;
And such the nature of the hallowed rite,
The wife her husband only could invite,
The slaves must all withdraw, and be debarred the
  sight.
Tereus, upon a throne of antique state,
Loftily raised, before the banquet sate;
And glutton-like luxuriously pleased,
With his own flesh his hungry maw appeased.
Nay, such a blindness o'er his senses falls,
That he for Itys to the table calls.
When Procne, now impatient to disclose
The joy that from her full revenge arose,
Cries out, in transports of a cruel mind,
'Within yourself your Itys you may find!'
Still at this puzzling answer, with surprise,
Around the room he sends his curious eyes;
And, as he still enquired, and called aloud,
Fierce Philomela, all besmeared with blood,
Her hands with murder stained, her spreading hair
Hanging dishevelled with a ghastly air,
Stepped forth, and flung full in the tyrant's face
The head of Itys, gory as it was:
Nor ever longed so much to use her tongue,
And with a just reproach to vindicate her wrong.
  The Thracian monarch from the table flings,
While with his cries the vaulted parlour rings;
His imprecations echo down to hell,
And rouse the snaky Furies from their Stygian cell.
One while he labours to disgorge his breast,
And free his stomach from the cursèd feast;
Then, weeping o'er his lamentable doom,
He styles himself his son's sepulchral tomb.
Now, with drawn sabre, and impetuous speed,

In close pursuit he drives Pandion's breed;
Whose nimble feet spring with so swift a force
Across the fields, they seem to wing their course.
And now, on real wings themselves they raise,
And steer their airy flight by different ways;
One to the woodland's shady covert hies,
Around the smoky roof the other flies;
Whose feathers yet the marks of murder stain,
Where, stamped upon her breast, the crimson spots
   remain.
Tereus, through grief and haste to be revenged,
Shares the like fate, and to a bird is changed:
Fixed on his head, the crested plumes appear,
Long is his beak, and sharpened like a spear;
Thus armed, his looks his inward mind display,
And, to a lapwing turned, he fans his way.


## from Book 8

### (1)

*Daedalus, having been employed by King Minos to build the
Labyrinth to house the Minotaur, longs to leave Crete, and plans to
fly back to his native Athens.*

In tedious exile now too long detained,
Daedalus languished for his native land;
The sea foreclosed his flight, yet thus he said:
'Though earth and water in subjection laid,
O cruel Minos, thy dominion be,
We'll go through air; for sure the air is free.'
Then to new arts his cunning thought applies,
And to improve the work of nature tries.
A row of quills in gradual order placed,

Rise by degrees in length from first to last;
As on a cliff th' ascending thicket grows,
Or different reeds the rural pipe compose.
Along the middle runs a twine of flax,
The bottom stems are joined by pliant wax.
Thus, well compact, a hollow bending brings
The fine composure into real wings.
  His boy, young Icarus, that near him stood,
Unthinking of his fate, with smiles pursued
The floating feathers, which the moving air
Bore loosely from the ground, and wafted here and
    there;
Or with the wax impertinently played,
And with his childish tricks the great design delayed.
  The final master-stroke at last imposed,
And now, the neat machine completely closed;
Fitting his pinions, on a flight he tries,
And hung self-balanced in the beaten skies.
Then thus instructs his child: 'My boy, take care
To wing your course along the middle air;
If low, the surges wet your flagging plumes,
If high, the sun the melting wax consumes.
Steer between both; nor to the northern skies,
Nor south Orion turn your giddy eyes;
But follow me: let me before you lay
Rules for the flight, and mark the pathless way.'
  Then teaching, with a fond concern, his son,
He took the untried wings, and fixed 'em on:
But fixed with trembling hands; and, as he speaks,
The tears roll gently down his agèd cheeks.
Then kissed, and in his arms embraced him fast,
But knew not this embrace must be the last.
And mounting upward, as he wings his flight,
Back on his charge he turns his aching sight;

As parent birds, when first their callow care
Leave the high nest to tempt the liquid air.
Then cheers him on, and oft, with fatal art,
Reminds the stripling to perform his part.
  These, as the angler at the silent brook,
Or mountain shepherd leaning on his crook,
Or gaping ploughman from the vale descries,
They stare and view 'em with religious eyes,
And straight conclude 'em gods; since none but they
Through their own azure skies could find a way.
  Now Delos, Paros on the left are seen,
And Samos, favoured by Jove's haughty queen;
Upon the right, the isle Lebynthos named,
And fair Calymne for its honey famed.
When now the boy, whose childish thoughts aspire
To loftier aims, and make him ramble higher,
Grown wild and wanton, more emboldened flies
Far from his guide, and soars among the skies.
The softening wax, that felt a nearer sun,
Dissolved apace, and soon began to run.
The youth in vain his melting pinions shakes,
His feathers gone, no longer air he takes.
'Oh, father, father!' as he strove to cry,
Down to the sea he tumbled from on high,
And found his fate; yet still subsists by fame,
Among those waters that retain his name.
  The father, now no more a father, cries,
'Ho, Icarus! Where are you?' as he flies.
'Where shall I seek my boy?' he cries again,
And saw his feathers scattered on the main.
Then cursed his art; and funeral rites conferred,
Naming the country from the youth interred.

                                   (trans. Samuel Croxall)

## (2)

*Baucis and Philemon, a worthy old couple, welcome into their cottage for a simple rural feast Jupiter and Mercury, who are visiting the earth incognito and who have been churlishly received elsewhere.*

From lofty roofs the gods repulsed before,
Now stooping entered through the little door:
The man (their hearty welcome first expressed)
A common settle drew for either guest,
Inviting each his weary limbs to rest.
But ere they sat, officious Baucis lays
Two cushions stuffed with straw, the seat to raise:
Coarse, but the best she had; then rakes the load
Of ashes from the hearth, and spreads abroad
The living coals; and, lest they should expire,
With leaves and bark she feeds her infant fire.
It smokes; and then with trembling breath she blows,
Till in a cheerful blaze the flames arose.
With brushwood, and with chips she strengthens these,
And adds at last the boughs of rotten trees.
The fire thus formed, she sets the kettle on,
(Like burnished gold the little seether shone);
Next took the coleworts which her husband got
From his own ground, a small well-watered spot;
She stripped the stalks of all their leaves; the best
She culled, and them with handy care she dressed.
High o'er the hearth a chine of bacon hung;
Good old Philemon seized it with a prong,
And from the sooty rafter drew it down,
Then cut a slice, but scarce enough for one;
Yet a large portion of a little store,
Which for their sakes alone he wished were more.
This in the pot he plunged without delay,

To tame the flesh, and drain the salt away.
The time between, before the fire they sat,
And shortened the delay by pleasing chat.
  A beam there was, on which a beechen pail
Hung by the handle, on a driven nail:
This filled with water, gently warmed, they set
Before their guests: in this they bathed their feet,
And after with clean towels dried their sweat.
This done, the host produced the genial bed,
Sallow the feet, the borders, and the stead,
Which with no costly coverlet they spread,
But coarse old garments; yet such robes as these
They laid alone at feasts, on holidays.
The good old housewife, tucking up her gown,
The table sets; th' invited gods lie down.
The trivet-table of a foot was lame,
A blot which prudent Baucis overcame,
Who thrusts beneath the limping leg a sherd,
So was the mended board exactly reared;
Then rubbed it o'er with newly gathered mint,
A wholesome herb that breathed a grateful scent.
Pallas began the feast, where first was seen
The particoloured olive, black and green:
Autumnal cornels next in order served,
In lees of wine well pickled and preserved.
A garden salad was the third supply,
Of endive, radishes and succory:
Then curds and cream, the flower of country fare,
And new-laid eggs, which Baucis' busy care
Turned by a gentle fire, and roasted rare.
All these in earthenware were served to board;
And next in place, an earthen pitcher stored,
With liquor of the best the cottage could afford.
This was the table's ornament and pride,

With figures wrought: like pages at his side
Stood beechen bowls; and these were shining clean,
Varnished with wax without, and lined within.
By this the boiling kettle had prepared,
And to the table sent the smoking lard;
On which with eager appetite they dine,
A savoury bit, that served to relish wine:
The wine itself was suiting to the rest,
Still working in the must, and lately pressed.
The second course succeeds like that before:
Plums, apples, nuts; and of their wintry store
Dry figs, and grapes, and wrinkled dates were set
In canisters, t' enlarge the little treat:
All these a milk-white honeycomb surround,
Which in the midst the country banquet crowned:
But the kind hosts their entertainment grace
With hearty welcome, and an open face:
In all they did, you might discern with ease
A willing mind, and a desire to please.

  Meantime the beechen bowls went round, and still,
Though often emptied, were observed to fill;
Filled without hands, and of their own accord
Ran without feet, and danced about the board.
Devotion seized the pair, to see the feast
With wine, and of no common grape, increased;
And up they held their hands, and fell to prayer,
Excusing, as they could, their country fare.
  One goose they had – 'twas all they could allow –
A wakeful sentry, and on duty now,
Whom to the gods for sacrifice they vow:
Her with malicious zeal the couple viewed;
She ran for life, and limping they pursued:
Full well the fowl perceived their bad intent,
And would not make her master's compliment;

But persecuted, to the powers she flies,
And close between the legs of Jove she lies:
He with a gracious ear the suppliant heard,
And saved her life; then what he was declared,
And owned the god. 'The neighbourhood,' said he,
'Shall justly perish for impiety:
You stand alone exempted; but obey
With speed, and follow where we lead the way:
Leave these accursed; and to the mountain's height
Ascend, nor once look backward in your flight.'

### (3)

*The gods destroy the neighbourhood in a flood, and transform Baucis'*
*and Philemon's cottage into a temple. They then grant the old couple*
*one wish.*

Awhile they whisper; then, to Jove addressed,
Philemon thus prefers their joint request:
'We crave to serve before your sacred shrine,
And offer at your altars rites divine:
And since not any action of our life
Has been polluted with domestic strife;
We beg one hour of death; that neither she
With widow's tears may live to bury me,
Nor weeping I, with withered arms may bear
My breathless Baucis to the sepulchre.'
  The godheads sign their suit. They run their race
In the same tenor all th' appointed space:
Then, when their hour was come, while they relate
These past adventures at the temple gate,
Old Baucis is by old Philemon seen
Sprouting with sudden leaves of sprightly green:
Old Baucis looked where old Philemon stood,
And saw his lengthened arms a sprouting wood:

New roots their fastened feet begin to bind,
Their bodies stiffen in a rising rind:
Then, ere the bark above their shoulders grew,
They give, and take at once their last adieu.
At once, 'Farewell, O faithful spouse,' they said;
At once th' encroaching rinds their closing lips invade.

(trans. John Dryden)

### (4)

*Erisichthon cuts down an oak sacred to Ceres. The goddess sends a mountain nymph to the abode of Famine in Scythia.*

There in a stony field the fiend she found,
Herbs gnawing, and roots scratching from the ground.
Her elf-lock hair in matted tresses grew,
Sunk were her eyes, and pale her ghastly hue,
Wan were her lips, and foul with clammy glue.
Her throat was furred, her guts appeared within
With snaky crawlings through her parchment skin.
Her jutting hips seemed starting from their place,
And for a belly was a belly's space.
Her dugs hung dangling from her craggy spine,
Loose to her breast, and fastened to her chine.
Her joints protuberant by leanness grown,
Consumption sunk the flesh, and raised the bone.
Her knees' large orbits bunched to monstrous size,
And ankles to undue proportion rise.

### (5)

*Famine infects Erisichthon in his sleep.*

Still slumbers Erisichthon's senses drown,
And soothe his fancy with their softest down.

He dreams of viands delicate to eat,
And revels on imaginary meat;
Chaws with his working mouth, but chaws in vain,
And tires his grinding teeth with fruitless pain;
Deludes his throat with visionary fare,
Feasts on the wind, and banquets on the air.
  The morning came, the night and slumbers past,
But still the furious pangs of hunger last;
The cankerous rage still gnaws with griping pains,
Stings in his throat, and in his bowels reigns.
Straight he requires, impatient in demand,
Provisions from the air, the seas, the land.
But though the land, air, seas provisions grant,
Starves at full tables, and complains of want.
What to a people might in dole be paid,
Or victual cities for a long blockade,
Could not one wolfish appetite assuage,
For glutting nourishment increased its rage.
As rivers poured from every distant shore,
The sea insatiate drinks, and thirsts for more;
Or as the fire, which all materials burns,
And wasted forests into ashes turns,
Grows more voracious, as the more it preys,
Recruits dilate the flame, and spread the blaze;
So impious Erisichthon's hunger raves,
Receives refreshments, and refreshments craves.
Food raises a desire for food, and meat
Is but a new provocative to eat.
He grows more empty, as the more supplied,
And endless cramming but extends the void …
At last all means, as all provisions failed;
For the disease by remedies prevailed.
His muscles with a furious bite he tore,
Gorged his own tattered flesh, and gulped his gore.

Wounds were his feast, his life to life a prey,
Supporting nature by its own decay.

(trans. Edward Vernon)

## from Book 10

### (1)

*Orpheus, desolate at the loss of his wife, Eurydice, now shuns female
company and sings to the trees. One of his songs is of Hyacinthus,
a Spartan youth loved by Apollo.*

Phoebus for thee too, Hyacinth, designed
A place among the gods, had fate been kind;
Yet this he gave: as oft as wintry rains
Are past, and vernal breezes soothe the plains,
From the green turf a purple flower you rise,
And with your fragrant breath perfume the skies.
  You when alive were Phoebus' darling boy;
In you he placed his heaven, and fixed his joy:
Their god the Delphic priests consult in vain;
Eurotas now he loves, and Sparta's plain:
His hands the use of bow and harp forget,
And hold the dogs, or bear the corded net;
O'er hanging cliffs swift he pursues the game;
Each hour his pleasure, each augments his flame.
  The midday sun now shone with equal light
Between the past and the succeeding night;
They strip, then, smoothed with suppling oil, essay
To pitch the rounded quoit, their wonted play.
A well-poised disk first hasty Phoebus threw,
It cleft the air, and whistled as it flew;
It reached the mark, a most surprising length;
Which spoke an equal share of art and strength.
Scarce was it fall'n, when with too eager hand

Young Hyacinth ran to snatch it from the sand;
But the cursed orb, which met a stony soil,
Flew in his face with violent recoil.
Both faint, both pale, and breathless now appear,
The boy with pain, the amorous god with fear.
He ran, and raised him bleeding from the ground,
Chafes his cold limbs, and wipes the fatal wound;
Then herbs of noblest juice in vain applies;
The wound is mortal, and his skill defies.
  As in a watered garden's blooming walk,
When some rude hand has bruised its tender stalk,
A fading lily droops its languid head,
And bends to earth, its life and beauty fled:
So Hyacinth, with head reclined, decays,
And, sickening, now no more his charms displays.
  'O thou art gone, my boy,' Apollo cried,
'Defrauded of thy youth in all its pride!
Thou, once my joy, art all my sorrow now;
And to my guilty hand my grief I owe.
Yet from myself I might the fault remove,
Unless to sport and play a fault should prove,
Unless it too were called a fault to love.
O could I for thee, or but with thee, die!
But cruel Fates to me that power deny.
Yet on my tongue thou shalt for ever dwell;
Thy name my lyre shall sound, my verse shall tell;
And to a flower transformed, unheard of yet,
Stamped on thy leaves my cries thou shalt repeat.
The time shall come, prophetic I foreknow,
When joined to thee a mighty chief shall grow,
And with my plaints his name thy leaf shall show.'
  While Phoebus thus the laws of fate revealed,
Behold, the blood which stained the verdant field
Is blood no longer, but a flower full blown

Far brighter than the Tyrian scarlet shone.
A lily's form it took; its purple hue
Was all that made a difference to the view.
Nor stopped he here; the god upon its leaves
The sad expression of his sorrow weaves;
And to this hour the mournful purple wears
'Ai, Ai', inscribed in funeral characters.
Nor are the Spartans, who so much are famed
For virtue, of their Hyacinth ashamed;
But still with pompous woe and solemn state,
The Hyacinthian feasts they yearly celebrate.

(trans. John Ozell)

## (2)

*Orpheus sings of Pygmalion, who, disgusted with women's conduct, resolves to remain single, but sculpts a maiden in ivory.*

Pygmalion, loathing their lascivious life,
Abhorred all womankind, but most a wife:
So single chose to live, and shunned to wed,
Well pleased to want a consort of his bed.
Yet fearing idleness, the nurse of ill,
In sculpture exercised his happy skill;
And carved in ivory such a maid, so fair,
As nature could not with his art compare,
Were she to work; but in her own defence
Must take her pattern here, and copy hence.
  Pleased with his idol, he commends, admires,
Adores, and, last, the thing adored desires.
A very virgin in her face was seen,
And had she moved, a living maid had been:
One would have thought she could have stirred, but
    strove
With modesty, and was ashamed to move.

Art hid with art, so well performed the cheat,
It caught the carver with his own deceit:
He knows 'tis madness, yet he must adore,
And still the more he knows it, loves the more;
The flesh, or what so seems, he touches oft,
Which feels so smooth that he believes it soft.
Fired with this thought, at once he strained the breast,
And on the lips a burning kiss impressed.
'Tis true, the hardened breast resists the gripe,
And the cold lips return a kiss unripe:
But when, retiring back, he looked again,
To think it ivory was a thought too mean:
So would believe she kissed, and, courting more,
Again embraced her naked body o'er;
And straining hard the statue, was afraid
His hands had made a dint, and hurt his maid;
Explored her limb by limb, and feared to find
So rude a gripe had left a livid mark behind.
With flattery now he seeks her mind to move,
And now with gifts, the powerful bribes of love,
He furnishes her closet first; and fills
The crowded shelves with rarities of shells;
Adds orient pearls, which from the conches he drew,
And all the sparkling stones of various hue;
And parrots, imitating human tongue,
And singing-birds in silver cages hung;
And every fragrant flower, and odorous green
Were sorted well, with lumps of amber laid between:
Rich fashionable robes her person deck,
Pendants her ears, and pearls adorn her neck;
Her tapered fingers, too, with rings are graced,
And an embroidered zone surrounds her slender waist.
Thus like a queen arrayed, so richly dressed,
Beauteous she showed, but naked showed the best.

Then from the floor, he raised a royal bed,
With coverings of Sidonian purple spread:
The solemn rites performed, he calls her bride,
With blandishments invites her to his side;
And as she were with vital sense possessed,
Her head did on a plumy pillow rest.

### (3)

*Pygmalion prays to Venus to have the 'likeness' of his 'ivory maid'.*
*She signals that his request will be granted.*

The youth returning to his mistress hies,
And impudent in hope, with ardent eyes
And beating breast, by the dear statue lies.
He kisses her white lips, renews the bliss,
And looks, and thinks they redden at the kiss;
He thought them warm before; nor longer stays,
But next his hand on her hard bosom lays:
Hard as it was, beginning to relent,
It seemed the breast beneath his fingers bent;
He felt again, his fingers made a print,
'Twas flesh, but flesh so firm it rose against the dint;
The pleasing task he fails not to renew;
Soft, and more soft at every touch it grew;
Like pliant wax, when chasing hands reduce
The former mass to form, and frame for use.
He would believe, but yet is still in pain,
And tries his argument of sense again,
Presses the pulse, and feels the leaping vein.
Convinced, o'erjoyed, his studied thanks and praise
To her who made the miracle he pays:
Then lips to lips he joined; now freed from fear,
He found the savour of the kiss sincere.
At this the wakened image oped her eyes,

And viewed at once the light and lover with surprise.
The goddess, present at the match she made,
So blessed the bed, such fruitfulness conveyed,
That ere ten months had sharpened either horn,
To crown their bliss a lovely boy was born;
Paphos his name, who, grown to manhood, walled
The city Paphos, from the founder called.

### (4)

*Orpheus next tells of Myrrha, a Cypriot princess consumed with incestuous passion for her father, Cinyras. She reflects on the paradoxes of her plight.*

'Ah Myrrha, whither would thy wishes tend?
Ye gods, ye sacred laws, my soul defend
From such a crime as all mankind detest,
And never lodged before in human breast!
But is it sin? Or makes my mind alone
Th' imagined sin? For Nature makes it none.
What tyrant then these envious laws began,
Made not for any other beast, but man?
The father-bull his daughter may bestride,
The horse may make his mother-mare a bride;
What piety forbids the lusty ram
Or more salacious goat to rut their dam?
The hen is free to wed the chick she bore,
And make a husband whom she hatched before.
All creatures else are of a happier kind,
Whom nor ill-natured laws from pleasure bind,
Nor thoughts of sin disturb their peace of mind.
But man a slave of his own making lives;
The fool denies himself what Nature gives:
Too busy senates, with an over-care
To make us better than our kind can bear,

Have dashed a spice of envy in the laws,
And straining up too high have spoiled the cause.
Yet some wise nations break their cruel chains,
And own no laws, but those which love ordains;
Where happy daughters with their sires are joined,
And piety is doubly paid in kind.
O that I had been born in such a clime,
Not here, where 'tis the country makes the crime!
  But whither would my impious fancy stray?
Hence hopes, and ye forbidden thoughts, away!
His worth deserves to kindle my desires,
But with the love that daughters bear to sires.
Then had not Cinyras my father been,
What hindered Myrrha's hopes to be his queen?
But the perverseness of my fate is such,
That he's not mine, because he's mine too much:
Our kindred blood debars a better tie;
He might be nearer, were he not so nigh.
Eyes and their objects never must unite,
Some distance is required to help the sight;
Fain would I travel to some foreign shore,
Never to see my native country more,
So might I to myself myself restore;
So might my mind these impious thoughts remove,
And ceasing to behold, might cease to love.
But stay I must, to feed my famished sight,
To talk, to kiss, and more, if more I might:
More, impious maid? What more canst thou design,
To make a monstrous mixture in thy line,
And break all statutes human and divine?
Can'st thou be called, to save thy wretched life,
Thy mother's rival and thy father's wife?
Confound so many sacred names in one,
Thy brother's mother? Sister to thy son?

And fear'st thou not to see th' infernal bands,
Their heads with snakes, with torches armed their
    hands;
Full at thy face th' avenging brands to bear,
And shake the serpents from their hissing hair?
But thou in time th' increasing ill control,
Nor first debauch the body by the soul;
Secure the sacred quiet of thy mind,
And keep the sanctions Nature has designed.
  Suppose I should attempt, th' attempt were vain,
No thoughts like mine, his sinless soul profane:
Observant of the right; and O that he
Could cure my madness, or be mad like me!'

(5)

*Having consummated her passion, Myrrha repents and asks to be
translated into a middle state between life and death. She is
transformed into a myrrh tree.*

The prayers of penitents are never vain;
At least she did her last request obtain:
For while she spoke, the ground began to rise,
And gathered round her feet, her legs, and thighs;
Her toes in roots descend, and spreading wide,
A firm foundation for the trunk provide:
Her solid bones convert to solid wood,
To pith her marrow, and to sap her blood;
Her arms are boughs, her fingers change their kind;
Her tender skin is hardened into rind.
  And now the rising tree her womb invests,
Now, shooting upwards still, invades her breasts,
And shades the neck; when, weary with delay,
She sunk her head within, and met it half the way.
And though with outward shape she lost her sense,

With bitter tears she wept her last offence;
And still she weeps, nor sheds her tears in vain;
For still the precious drops her name retain.

(trans. John Dryden)


## from Book 11

### (1)

*The Bacchantes attack Orpheus for maligning the female sex.*

Here, while the Thracian bard's enchanting strain
Soothes beasts, and woods, and all the listening plain,
The female Bacchanals, devoutly mad,
In shaggy skins like savage creatures clad,
Warbling in air perceived his lovely lay,
And from a rising ground beheld him play.
When one, the wildest, with dishevelled hair
That loosely streamed and ruffled in the air,
Soon as her frantic eye the lyrist spied,
'See, see, the hater of our sex!' she cried,
Then at his face her missive javelin sent,
Which whizzed along, and brushed him as it went;
But the soft wreaths of ivy twisted round
Prevent a deep impression of the wound.
Another for a weapon hurls a stone,
Which, by the sound subdued as soon as thrown,
Falls at his feet, and with a seeming sense
Implores his pardon for its late offence.
  But now their frantic rage unbounded grows,
Turns all to madness, and no measure knows:
Yet this the charms of music might subdue;
But that, with all its charms, is conquered too.
In louder strains their hideous yellings rise,

And squeaking hornpipes echo through the skies,
Which, in hoarse consort with the drum, confound
The moving lyre and every gentle sound.
  Then 'twas the deafened stones flew on with speed,
And saw, unsoothed, their tuneful poet bleed.
The birds, the beasts, and all the savage crew
Which the sweet lyrist to attention drew,
Now, by the female mob's more furious rage,
Are driv'n, and forced to quit the shady stage.
Next their fierce hands the bard himself assail,
Nor can his song against their wrath prevail:
They flock like birds, when, in a clustering flight,
By day they chase the boding fowl of night.
So crowded amphitheatres survey
The stag to greedy dogs a future prey.
Their steely javelins, which soft curls entwine
Of budding tendrils from the leafy vine,
For sacred rites of mild religion made,
Are flung promiscuous at the poet's head.
Those clods of earth or flints discharge, and these
Hurl prickly branches slivered from the trees.
And, lest their passion should be unsupplied,
The rabble crew, by chance, at distance spied
Where oxen, straining at the heavy yoke,
The fallowed field with slow advances broke;
Nigh which the brawny peasants dug the soil,
Procuring food with long laborious toil.
These, when they saw the ranting throng draw near,
Quitted their tools, and fled possessed with fear.
Long spades and rakes of mighty size were found,
Carelessly left upon the broken ground.
With these the furious lunatics engage,
And first the labouring oxen feel their rage;
Then to the poet they return with speed,

Whose fate was past prevention now decreed:
In vain he lifts his suppliant hands, in vain
He tries, before, his never-failing strain.
And, from those sacred lips, whose thrilling sound
Fierce tigers and insensate rocks could wound,
Ah gods, how moving was the mournful sight!
To see the fleeting soul now take its flight.
Thee the soft warblers of the feathered kind
Bewailed; for thee thy savage audience pined;
Those rocks and woods that oft thy strain had led,
Mourn for their charmer, and lament him dead;
And drooping trees their leafy glories shed.
Naiads and Dryads with dishevelled hair
Promiscuous weep, and scarves of sable wear;
Nor could the river gods conceal their moan,
But with new floods of tears augment their own.
 His mangled limbs lay scattered all around,
His head and harp a better fortune found;
In Hebrus' streams they gently rolled along,
And soothed the waters with a mournful song.
Soft deadly notes the lifeless tongue inspire,
A doleful tune sounds from the floating lyre;
The hollow banks in solemn consort mourn,
And the sad strain in echoing groans return.
Now with the current to the sea they glide,
Borne by the billows of the briny tide;
And driv'n where waves round rocky Lesbos roar,
They strand, and lodge upon Methymna's shore.
 But here, when landed on the foreign soil,
A venomed snake, the product of the isle,
Attempts the head, and sacred locks embrued
With clotted gore, and still fresh dropping blood.
Phoebus, at last, his kind protection gives,
And from the fact the greedy monster drives:

Whose marbled jaws his impious crime atone,
Still grinning ghastly, though transformed to stone.
  His ghost flies downward to the Stygian shore,
And knows the places it had seen before:
Among the shadows of the pious train
He finds Eurydice, and loves again;
With pleasure views the beauteous phantom's charms,
And clasps her in his unsubstantial arms.
There side by side they unmolested walk,
Or pass their blissful hours in pleasing talk;
Aft or before the bard securely goes,
And, without danger, can review his spouse.

### (2)

*Bacchus offers to grant King Midas one wish. Midas asks that
everything he touches be converted to gold.*

But the brave king departed from the place,
With smiles of gladness sparkling in his face;
Nor could contain, but, as he took his way,
Impatient longs to make the first essay.
Down from a lowly branch a twig he drew,
The twig straight glittered with a golden hue:
He takes a stone, the stone was turned to gold;
A clod he touches, and the crumbling mould
Acknowledged soon the great transforming power,
In weight and substance like a mass of ore.
He plucked the corn, and straight his grasp appears
Filled with a bending tuft of golden ears.
An apple next he takes, and seems to hold
The bright, Hesperian vegetable gold.
His hand he careless on a pillar lays,
With shining gold the fluted pillars blaze:
And while he washes, as the servants pour,

His touch converts the stream to Danaë's shower.
  To see these miracles so finely wrought,
Fires with transporting joy his giddy thought.
The ready slaves prepare a sumptuous board,
Spread with rich dainties for their happy lord;
Whose powerful hands the bread no sooner hold,
But its whole substance is transformed to gold.
Up to his mouth he lifts the savoury meat,
Which turns to gold as he attempts to eat:
His patron's noble juice of purple hue,
Touched by his lips, a gilded cordial grew;
Unfit for drink, and wondrous to behold,
It trickles from his jaws a fluid gold.

### (3)

*Midas repents of his wish, and Bacchus transfers the king's golden touch to a river which henceforth has a bed of golden sand. The rustic god Pan challenges Apollo to a singing contest. The discerning members of the audience prefer Apollo, but Midas votes for Pan — for which he receives an appropriate punishment.*

The lyric god, who thought his untuned ear
Deserved but ill a human form to wear,
Of that deprives him, and supplies the place
With some more fit, and of an ampler space:
Fixed on his noddle an unseemly pair,
Flagging, and large, and full of whitish hair;
Without a total change from what he was,
Still in the man preserve the simple ass.
  He, to conceal the scandal of the deed,
A purple turban folds about his head;
Veils the reproach from public view, and fears
The laughing world would spy his monstrous ears.
One trusty barber-slave, that used to dress

His master's hair when lengthened to excess,
The mighty secret knew, but knew alone,
And, though impatient, durst not make it known.
Restless, at last, a private place he found,
Then dug a hole and told it to the ground;
In a low whisper he revealed the case,
And covered in the earth, and silent left the place.
  In time, of trembling reeds a plenteous crop
From the confided furrow sprouted up;
Which, high advancing with the ripening year,
Made known the tiller and his fruitless care:
For then the rustling blades and whispering wind
To tell th' important secret both combined.

                                        (trans. Samuel Croxall)


### (4)

*Ceyx, son of Lucifer and king of Trachis, is warned by his wife*
*Alcyone, daughter of Aeolus, not to go on a sea voyage. Her fears*
*prove justified, when his ship is caught in a storm.*

Now waves on waves ascending scale the skies,
And in the fires above the water fries:
When yellow sands are sifted from below,
The glittering billows give a golden show:
And when the fouler bottom spews the black,
The Stygian dye the tainted waters take:
Then frothy white appear the flatted seas,
And change their colour, changing their disease.
Like various fits the Trachin vessel finds,
And now sublime, she rides upon the winds;
As from a lofty summit looks from high,
And from the clouds beholds the nether sky;
Now from the depth of hell they lift their sight,
And at a distance see superior light:

The lashing billows make a loud report,
And beat her sides, as battering rams a fort;
Or as a lion bounding in his way,
With force augmented, bears against his prey,
Sidelong to seize; or unappalled with fear,
Springs on the toils, and rushes on the spear:
So seas impelled by winds, with added power
Assault the sides, and o'er the hatches tower.

  The planks, their pitchy covering washed away,
Now yield; and now a yawning breach display;
The roaring waters with a hostile tide
Rush through the ruins of her gaping side.
Meantime in sheets of rain the sky descends,
And ocean swelled with waters upwards tends;
One rising, falling one, the heavens and sea
Meet at their confines, in the middle way:
The sails are drunk with showers, and drop with rain,
Sweet waters mingle with the briny main.
No star appears to lend his friendly light;
Darkness and tempest make a double night;
But flashing fires disclose the deep by turns,
And while the lightnings blaze, the water burns.

  Now all the waves their scattered force unite,
And as a soldier, foremost in the fight,
Makes way for others, and an host alone
Still presses on, and urging gains the town;
So while th' invading billows come abreast,
The hero tenth advanced before the rest,
Sweeps all before him with impetuous sway,
And from the walls descends upon the prey;
Part following enter, part remain without,
With envy hear their fellows' conquering shout,
And mount on others' backs, in hope to share
The city, thus become the seat of war.

### (5)

*Ceyx drowns, thinking of Alcyone.*

Ev'n he who late a sceptre did command,
Now grasps a floating fragment in his hand;
And while he struggles on the stormy main,
Invokes his father, and his wife's, in vain.
But yet his consort is his greatest care;
Alcyone he names amidst his prayer;
Names as a charm against the waves and wind;
Most in his mouth, and ever in his mind.
Tired with his toil, all hopes of safety past,
From prayers to wishes he descends at last;
That his dead body, wafted to the sands,
Might have its burial from her friendly hands.
As oft as he can catch a gulp of air,
And peep above the seas, he names the fair;
And ev'n when plunged beneath, on her he raves,
Murm'ring Alcyone below the waves:
At last a falling billow stops his breath,
Breaks o'er his head, and whelms him underneath.
Bright Lucifer unlike himself appears
That night, his heavenly form obscured with tears;
And since he was forbid to leave the skies,
He muffled with a cloud his mournful eyes.

### (6)

*At Juno's request, Iris visits the Cave of Sleep for a dream to inform
Alcyone of Ceyx's fate.*

Near the Cimmerians, in his dark abode,
Deep in a cavern, dwells the drowsy god;
Whose gloomy mansion nor the rising sun,
Nor setting, visits, nor the lightsome noon;

But lazy vapours round the region fly,
Perpetual twilight, and a doubtful sky.
No crowing cock does there his wings display,
Nor with his horny bill provoke the day;
Nor watchful dogs, nor the more wakeful geese,
Disturb with nightly noise the sacred peace;
Nor beast of nature, nor the tame are nigh,
Nor trees with tempests rocked, nor human cry;
But safe repose without an air of breath
Dwells here, and a dumb quiet next to death.

An arm of Lethe, with a gentle flow
Arising upwards from the rock below,
The palace moats, and o'er the pebbles creeps,
And with soft murmurs calls the coming sleeps.
Around its entry nodding poppies grow,
And all cool simples that sweet rest bestow;
Night from the plants their sleepy virtue drains,
And passing, sheds it on the silent plains;
No door there was th' unguarded house to keep,
On creaking hinges turned, to break his sleep.

But in the gloomy court was raised a bed,
Stuffed with black plumes, and on an ebon stead:
Black was the covering too, where lay the god,
And slept supine, his limbs displayed abroad:
About his head fantastic visions fly,
Which various images of things supply,
And mock their forms; the leaves on trees not more,
Nor bearded ears in fields, nor sands upon the shore.

The virgin entering bright, indulged the day
To the brown cave, and brushed the dreams away:
The god disturbed with this new glare of light,
Cast sudden on his face, unsealed his sight,
And raised his tardy head, which sunk again,
And sinking, on his bosom knocked his chin;

At length shook off himself, and asked the dame,
(And asking yawned) for what intent she came.
  To whom the goddess thus: 'O sacred rest,
Sweet pleasing sleep, of all the powers the best!
O peace of mind, repairer of decay,
Whose balms renew the limbs to labours of the day;
Care shuns thy soft approach, and sullen flies away!
Adorn a dream, expressing human form,
The shape of him who suffered in the storm,
And send it flitting to the Trachin court,
The wreck of wretched Ceyx to report:
Before his queen bid the pale spectre stand,
Who begs a vain relief at Juno's hand.'
She said, and scarce awake her eyes could keep,
Unable to support the fumes of sleep;
But fled, returning by the way she went,
And swerved along her bow with swift ascent.


## (7)

*Having heard of Ceyx's death, Alcyone goes to the shore, where she sees Ceyx's corpse drifting towards her. Resolved on death, she leaps from the harbourside.*

Headlong from hence to plunge herself she springs,
But shoots along supported on her wings;
A bird new-made about the banks she plies,
Not far from shore, and short excursions tries;
Nor seeks in air her humble flight to raise,
Content to skim the surface of the seas.
Her bill, though slender, sends a creaking noise,
And imitates a lamentable voice.
Now lighting where the bloodless body lies,
She with a funeral note renews her cries;
At all her stretch her little wings she spread,

And with her feathered arms embraced the dead:
Then flickering to his pallid lips, she strove
To print a kiss, the last essay of love.
Whether the vital touch revived the dead,
Or that the moving waters raised his head
To meet the kiss, the vulgar doubt alone;
For sure a present miracle was shown.
The gods their shapes to winter birds translate,
But both obnoxious to their former fate.
Their conjugal affection still is tied,
And still the mournful race is multiplied:
They bill, they tread; Alcyone compressed,
Sev'n days sits brooding on her floating nest,
A wintry queen. Her sire at length is kind,
Calms every storm, and hushes every wind;
Prepares his empire for his daughter's ease,
And for his hatching nephews smooths the seas.

## from Book 13

### (1)

*After the death of Achilles at the siege of Troy, a dispute arises
between the brawny Ajax and the quick-witted Ulysses as to who
shall inherit Achilles' arms. Ajax disputes Ulysses' claim, on the
grounds that Ulysses is a coward.*

'As next of kin Achilles' arms I claim;
This fellow would engraft a foreign name
Upon our stock, and the Sisyphian seed
By fraud and theft asserts his father's breed:
Then must I lose these arms, because I came
To fight uncalled, a voluntary name,
Nor shunned the cause, but offered you my aid,

While he long lurking was to war betrayed:
Forced to the field he came, but in the rear;
And feigned distraction to conceal his fear,
Till one more cunning caught him in the snare
(Ill for himself!) and dragged him into war.
Now let a hero's arms a coward vest,
And he who shunned all honours gain the best:
And let me stand excluded from my right,
Robbed of my kinsman's arms, who first appeared in
    fight.
Better for us, at home had he remained,
Had it been true the madness which he feigned,
Or so believed; the less had been our shame,
The less his counselled crime, which brands the
    Grecian name;
Nor Philoctetes had been left enclosed
In a bare isle, to wants and pains exposed,
Where to the rocks, with solitary groans,
His sufferings and our baseness he bemoans;
And wishes – so may heaven his wish fulfil! –
The due reward to him who caused his ill.
Now he, with us to Troy's destruction sworn,
Our brother of the war, by whom are borne
Alcides' arrows, pent in narrow bounds,
With cold and hunger pinched, and pained with
    wounds,
To find him food and clothing, must employ
Against the birds the shafts due to the fate of Troy.
Yet still he lives, and lives from treason free,
Because he left Ulysses' company;
Poor Palamede might wish, so void of aid,
Rather to have been left, than so to death betrayed:
The coward bore the man immortal spite,
Who shamed him out of madness into fight;

Nor daring otherwise to vent his hate,
Accused him first of treason to the state;
And then for proof produced the golden store,
Himself had hidden in his tent before:
Thus of two champions he deprived our host,
By exile one, and one by treason lost.
Thus fights Ulysses, thus his fame extends,
A formidable man, but to his friends.'

### (2)

*In his own speech, Ulysses responds to Ajax's charges.*

'Beside, what wise objections he prepares
Against my late accession to the wars!
Does not the fool perceive his argument
Is with more force against Achilles bent?
For if dissembling be so great a crime,
The fault is common, and the same in him:
And if he taxes both of long delay,
My guilt is less, who sooner came away.
His pious mother, anxious for his life,
Detained her son; and me, my pious wife.
To them the blossoms of our youth were due,
Our riper manhood we reserved for you.
But grant me guilty, 'tis not much my care,
When with so great a man my guilt I share:
My wit to war the matchless hero brought,
But by this fool I never had been caught.
  Nor need I wonder that on me he threw
Such foul aspersions, when he spares not you:
If Palamede unjustly fell by me,
Your honour suffered in th' unjust decree:
I but accused, you doomed: and yet he died,
Convinced of treason, and was fairly tried:

You heard not he was false; your eyes beheld
The traitor manifest, the bribe revealed.
  That Philoctetes is on Lemnos left,
Wounded, forlorn, of human aid bereft,
Is not my crime, or not my crime alone;
Defend your justice, for the fact's your own:
'Tis true, th' advice was mine; that staying there
He might his weary limbs with rest repair,
From a long voyage free, and from a longer war.
He took the counsel, and he lives at least;
Th' event declares I counselled for the best:
Though faith is all, in ministers of state;
For who can promise to be fortunate?
Now since his arrows are the fate of Troy,
Do not my wit, or weak address, employ;
Send Ajax there, with his persuasive sense,
To mollify the man, and draw him thence:
But Xanthus shall run backward, Ida stand
A leafless mountain, and the Grecian band
Shall fight for Troy, if, when my counsel fail,
The wit of heavy Ajax can prevail!
  Hard Philoctetes, exercise thy spleen
Against thy fellows, and the king of men;
Curse my devoted head, above the rest,
And wish in arms to meet me breast to breast:
Yet I the dangerous task will undertake,
And either die myself, or bring thee back.'


### (3)

*The cyclops Polyphemus woos the water-nymph Galatea and reveals his jealousy of her lover, Acis.*

'The flocks you see are all my own; beside
The rest that woods and winding valleys hide,

And those that folded in the caves abide.
Ask not the numbers of my growing store;
Who knows how many, knows he has no more.
Nor will I praise my cattle; trust not me,
But judge yourself, and pass your own decree:
Behold their swelling dugs; the sweepy weight
Of ewes that sink beneath the milky freight!
In the warm folds their tender lambkins lie;
Apart from kids, that call with human cry.
New milk in nut-brown bowls is duly served
For daily drink; the rest for cheese reserved.
Nor are these household dainties all my store:
The fields and forests will afford us more;
The deer, the hare, the goat, the savage boar.
All sorts of venison, and of birds the best:
A pair of turtles taken from the nest.
I walked the mountains, and two cubs I found,
(Whose dam had left 'em on the naked ground)
So like, that no distinction could be seen:
So pretty, they were presents for a queen;
And so they shall; I took 'em both away,
And keep, to be companions of your play.

  O raise, fair nymph, your beauteous face above
The waves, nor scorn my presents and my love!
Come, Galatea, come, and view my face;
I late beheld it, in the watery glass,
And found it lovelier than I feared it was.
Survey my towering stature, and my size:
Not Jove, the Jove you dream that rules the skies,
Bears such a bulk, or is so largely spread:
My locks – the plenteous harvest of my head –
Hang o'er my manly face, and, dangling down,
As with a shady grove, my shoulders crown.
Nor think, because my limbs and body bear

A thickset underwood of bristling hair,
My shape deformed; what fouler sight can be,
Than the bald branches of a leafless tree?
Foul is the steed, without a flowing mane,
And birds, without their feathers and their train.
Wool decks the sheep, and man receives a grace
From bushy limbs, and from a bearded face.
My forehead with a single eye is filled,
Round as a ball, and ample as a shield.
The glorious lamp of heaven, the radiant sun,
Is Nature's eye; and she's content with one.
Add, that my father sways your seas, and I,
Like you, am of the watery family.
I make you his, in making you my own;
You I adore, and kneel to you alone;
Jove with his fabled thunder I despise,
And only fear the lightning of your eyes.
Frown not, fair nymph; yet I could bear to be
Disdained, if others were disdained with me.
But to repulse the cyclops, and prefer
The love of Acis – heavens, I cannot bear!
But let the stripling please himself; nay more,
Please you – though that's the thing I most abhor;
The boy shall find, if e'er we cope in fight,
These giant limbs endued with giant might.
His living bowels, from his belly torn,
And scattered limbs shall on the flood be borne:
Thy flood, ungrateful nymph; and fate shall find
That way for thee and Acis to be joined.
For oh, I burn with love, and thy disdain
Augments at once my passion, and my pain!
Translated Etna flames within my heart,
And thou, inhuman, wilt not ease my smart.'

(trans. John Dryden)

## from Book 14

*The Hamadryad Pomona is wooed by the rural god Vertumnus.*

A Hamadryad flourished in these days,
Her name Pomona, from her woodland race.
In garden culture none could so excel,
Or form the pliant souls of plants so well;
Or to the fruit more generous flavours lend,
Or teach the trees with nobler loads to bend.

  The nymph frequented not the flattering stream,
Nor meads, the subject of a virgin's dream;
But to such joys her nursery did prefer,
Alone to tend her vegetable care.
A pruning hook she carried in her hand,
And taught the stragglers to obey command;
Lest the licentious and unthrifty bough,
The too indulgent parent should undo.
She shows how stocks invite to their embrace
A graft, and naturalize a foreign race
To mend the savage taint; and in its stead
Adopt new nature, and a nobler breed.

  Now hourly she observes her growing care,
And guards their nonage from the bleaker air:
Then opes her streaming sluices, to supply
With flowing draughts her thirsty family.

  Long had she laboured to continue free
From chains of love and nuptial tyranny;
And in her orchard's small extent immured,
Her vowed virginity she still secured.
Oft would loose Pan and all the lustful train
Of satyrs tempt her innocence in vain.
Silenus, that old dotard, owned a flame;
And he, that frights the thieves with stratagem
Of sword, and something else too gross to name.

Vertumnus too pursued the maid no less;
But with his rivals shared a like success.
To gain access a thousand ways he tries;
Oft in the hind the lover would disguise.
The heedless lout comes shambling on, and seems
Just sweating from the labour of his teams.
Then from the harvest oft the mimic swain
Seems bending with a load of bearded grain.
Sometimes a dresser of the vine he feigns,
And lawless tendrils to their bounds restrains.
Sometimes his sword a soldier shows; his rod
An angler; still so various is the god.
Now in a forehead-cloth, some crone he seems,
A staff supplying the defect of limbs;
Admittance thus he gains; admires the store
Of fairest fruit; the fair possessor more;
Then greets her with a kiss; th' unpractised dame
Admired a grandame kissed with such a flame.
Now, seated by her, he beholds a vine
Around an elm in amorous foldings twine.
'If that fair elm,' he cried, 'alone should stand,
No grapes would glow with gold, and tempt the hand;
Or if that vine without her elm should grow,
'Twould creep a poor neglected shrub below.
Be then, fair nymph, by these examples led;
Nor shun, for fancied fears, the nuptial bed.
Not she for whom the Lapithites took arms,
Nor Sparta's queen could boast such heavenly charms.
And if you would on woman's faith rely,
None can your choice direct so well as I.
Though old, so much Pomona I adore,
Scarce does the bright Vertumnus love her more.
'Tis your fair self alone his breast inspires
With softest wishes, and unsoiled desires.

Then fly all vulgar followers, and prove
The god of seasons only worth your love.
On my assurance well you may repose;
Vertumnus scarce Vertumnus better knows.
True to his choice, all looser flames he flies;
Nor for new faces fashionably dies.
The charms of youth, and every smiling grace
Bloom in his features, and the god confess.
Besides, he puts on every shape at ease;
But those the most, that best Pomona please.
Still to oblige her is her lover's aim;
Their likings and aversions are the same.
Nor the fair fruit your burdened branches bear;
Nor all the youthful product of the year,
Could bribe his choice; yourself alone can prove
A fit reward for so refined a love.
Relent, fair nymph, and with a kind regret,
Think 'tis Vertumnus weeping at your feet.
A tale attend, through Cyprus known, to prove
How Venus once revenged neglected love.

  Iphis, of vulgar birth, by chance had viewed
Fair Anaxarete of Teucer's blood.
Not long had he beheld the royal dame,
Ere the bright sparkle kindled into flame.
Oft did he struggle with a just despair,
Unfixed to ask, unable to forbear.
But love, who flatters still his own disease,
Hopes all things will succeed, he knows will please.
Where'er the fair one haunts, he hovers there;
And seeks her confident with sighs and prayer,
Or letters he conveys, that seldom prove
Successless messengers in suits of love.

  Now shivering at her gates the wretch appears,
And myrtle garlands on the columns rears,

Wet with a deluge of unbidden tears.
The nymph more hard than rocks, more deaf than seas,
Derides his prayers; insults his agonies;
Arraigns of insolence th' aspiring swain;
And takes a cruel pleasure in his pain.
Resolved at last to finish his despair,
He thus upbraids th' inexorable fair:
"O Anaxarete, at last forget
The licence of a passion indiscreet.
Now triumph, since a welcome sacrifice
Your slave prepares, to offer to your eyes.
My life, without reluctance, I resign;
That present best can please a pride like thine.
But oh, forbear to blast a flame so bright,
Doomed never to expire, but with the light.
And you, great powers, do justice to my name;
The hours, you take from life, restore to fame."
  Then o'er the posts, once hung with wreaths, he
      throws
The ready cord, and fits the fatal noose;
For death prepares; and bounding from above,
At once the wretch concludes his life and love.
Ere long the people gather, and the dead
Is to his mourning mother's arms conveyed.
First like some ghastly statue she appears;
Then bathes the breathless corpse in seas of tears;
And gives it to the pile; now as the throng
Proceed in sad solemnity along,
To view the passing pomp the cruel fair
Hastes, and beholds her breathless lover there.
Struck with the sight, inanimate she seems;
Set are her eyes, and motionless her limbs:
Her features without fire, her colour gone,
And, like her heart, she hardens into stone.

In Salamis the statue still is seen
In the famed temple of the Cyprian queen.
Warned by this tale, no longer then disdain,
O nymph beloved, to ease a lover's pain.
So may the frosts in spring your blossoms spare,
And winds their rude autumnal rage forbear.'
  The story oft Vertumnus urged in vain,
But then assumed his heavenly form again.
Such looks and lustre the bright youth adorn,
As when with rays glad Phoebus paints the morn.
The sight so warms the fair admiring maid,
Like snow she melts: so soon can youth persuade.
Consent, on eager wings, succeeds desire,
And both the lovers glow with mutual fire.

(trans. Sir Samuel Garth)

## from Book 15

### (1)

*An old man of Crotona reports the Greek philosopher Pythagoras'
discourse on the transmigration of souls and the flux of nature.*

Then death, so called, is but old matter dressed
In some new figure, and a varied vest;
Thus all things are but altered, nothing dies;
And here and there th' unbodied spirit flies,
By time, or force, or sickness dispossessed,
And lodges, where it lights, in man or beast;
Or hunts without, till ready limbs it find,
And actuates those according to their kind;
From tenement to tenement is tossed,
The soul is still the same, the figure only lost:
And, as the softened wax new seals receives,

This face assumes, and that impression leaves;
Now called by one, now by another name;
The form is only changed, the wax is still the same:
So death, so called, can but the form deface;
Th' immortal soul flies out in empty space,
To seek her fortune in some other place.

  Then let not piety be put to flight,
To please the taste of glutton appetite;
But suffer inmate souls secure to dwell,
Lest from their seats your parents you expel;
With rabid hunger feed upon your kind,
Or from a beast dislodge a brother's mind.

  And since, like Tiphys parting from the shore,
In ample seas I sail, and depths untried before,
This let me further add, that nature knows
No steadfast station, but or ebbs or flows:
Ever in motion, she destroys her old,
And casts new figures in another mould.
Ev'n times are in perpetual flux, and run
Like rivers from their fountain, rolling on.
For time no more than streams is at a stay;
The flying hour is ever on her way:
And as the fountain still supplies her store,
The wave behind impels the wave before;
Thus in successive course the minutes run,
And urge their predecessor minutes on,
Still moving, ever new: for former things
Are set aside, like abdicated kings:
And every moment alters what is done,
And innovates some act till then unknown ...

  Perceiv'st thou not the process of the year,
How the four seasons in four forms appear,
Resembling human life in every shape they wear?
Spring first, like infancy, shoots out her head,

With milky juice requiring to be fed:
Helpless, though fresh, and wanting to be led.
The green stem grows in stature and in size,
But only feeds with hope the farmer's eyes;
Then laughs the childish year with flowrets crowned,
And lavishly perfumes the fields around,
But no substantial nourishment receives:
Infirm the stalks, unsolid are the leaves.
Proceeding onward whence the year began,
The summer grows adult, and ripens into man.
This season, as in men, is most replete
With kindly moisture and prolific heat.
Autumn succeeds, a sober, tepid age,
Not froze with fear, nor boiling into rage;
More than mature, and tending to decay,
When our brown locks repine to mix with odious
    grey.
Last, winter creeps along with tardy pace,
Sour is his front, and furrowed is his face;
His scalp if not dishonoured quite of hair,
The ragged fleece is thin; and thin is worse than bare.
  Ev'n our own bodies daily change receive;
Some part of what was theirs before they leave,
Nor are today what yesterday they were;
Nor the whole same tomorrow will appear.
  Time was when we were sowed, and just began,
From some few fruitful drops, the promise of a man:
Then Nature's hand – fermented as it was –
Moulded to shape the soft, coagulated mass;
And when the little man was fully formed,
The breathless embryo with a spirit warmed;
But when the mother's throes begin to come,
The creature, pent within the narrow room,
Breaks his blind prison, pushing to repair

His stifled breath, and draw the living air;
Cast on the margin of the world he lies,
A helpless babe, but by instinct he cries.
He next essays to walk, but downward pressed
On four feet imitates his brother beast;
By slow degrees he gathers from the ground
His legs, and to the rolling chair is bound;
Then walks alone; a horseman now become,
He rides a stick, and travels round the room;
In time he vaunts among his youthful peers;
Strong-boned, and strung with nerves, in pride of
    years,
He runs with mettle his first merry stage,
Maintains the next, abated of his rage,
But manages his strength, and spares his age.
Heavy the third, and stiff, he sinks apace,
And though 'tis downhill all, but creeps along the race.
Now sapless on the verge of death he stands,
Contemplating his former feet, and hands;
And Milo-like, his slackened sinews sees,
And withered arms, once fit to cope with Hercules,
Unable now to shake, much less to tear, the trees.

                         (trans. John Dryden)


## (2)

*Jupiter reassures Venus that Augustus, adopted son of the assassinated Julius Caesar, will triumph. Caesar's soul is stellified, and Ovid ends the Metamorphoses with a prediction of the poem's immortality.*

'He, goddess, for whose death the Fates you blame,
Has finished his determined course with fame:
To thee 'tis giv'n, at length, that he shall shine
Among the gods, and grace the worshipped shrine:
His son to all his greatness shall be heir,

And worthily succeed to empire's care:
Ourself will lead his wars, resolved to aid
The brave avenger of his father's shade:
To him its freedom Mutina shall owe,
And Decius his auspicious conduct know:
His dreadful powers shall shake Pharsalia's plain,
And drench in gore Philippi's fields again:
A mighty leader, in Sicilia's flood,
Great Pompey's warlike son shall be subdued:
Egypt's soft queen, adorned with fatal charms,
Shall mourn her soldier's unsuccessful arms;
Too late shall find her swelling hopes were vain,
And know that Rome o'er Memphis still must reign:
What name I Afric or Nile's hidden head?
Far as both oceans roll, his power shall spread:
All the known earth to him shall homage pay,
And the seas own his universal sway:
When cruel war no more disturbs mankind,
To civil studies shall he bend his mind,
With equal justice guardian laws ordain,
And by his great example vice restrain:
Where will his bounty or his goodness end?
To times unborn his generous views extend;
The virtues of his heir our praise engage,
And promise blessings to the coming age:
Late shall he in his kindred orbs be placed,
With Pylian years and crowded honours graced.
  Meantime, your hero's fleeting spirit bear,
Fresh from his wounds, and change it to a star:
So shall great Julius rites divine assume,
And from the skies eternal smile on Rome.'
  This spoke, the goddess to the Senate flew;
Where, her fair form concealed from mortal view,
Her Caesar's heavenly part she made her care,

Nor left the recent soul to waste to air;
But bore it upwards to its native skies:
Glowing with new-born fires she saw it rise;
Forth springing from her bosom up it flew,
And, kindling as it soared, a comet grew;
Above the lunar sphere it took its flight
And shot behind it a long trail of light.

Thus raised, his glorious offspring Julius viewed,
Beneficently great, and scattering good;
Deeds that his own surpassed with joy beheld,
And his large heart dilates to be excelled.
What though this prince refuses to receive
The preference which his juster subjects give;
Fame uncontrolled, that no restraint obeys,
The homage shunned by modest virtue pays,
And proves disloyal only in his praise.
Though great his sire, him greater we proclaim:
So Atreus yields to Agamemnon's fame;
Achilles so superior honours won,
And Peleus must submit to Peleus' son;
Examples yet more noble to disclose,
So Saturn was eclipsed, when Jove to empire rose:
Jove rules the heav'ns, the earth Augustus sways;
Each claims a monarch's and a father's praise.

Celestials, who for Rome your cares employ;
Ye gods who guarded the remains of Troy;
Ye native gods, here born and fixed by Fate;
Quirinus, founder of the Roman state;
O parent Mars, from whom Quirinus sprung;
Chaste Vesta, Caesar's household gods among
Most sacred held; domestic Phoebus, thou,
To whom with Vesta chaste alike we bow;
Great guardian of the high Tarpeian rock;
And all ye powers whom poets may invoke;

O grant, that day may claim our sorrows late,
When loved Augustus shall submit to Fate,
Visit those seats where gods and heroes dwell,
And leave in tears the world he ruled so well!
  The work is finished, which nor dreads the rage
Of tempests, fire, or war, or wasting age:
Come, soon or late, death's undetermined day,
This mortal being only can decay;
My nobler part, my fame, shall reach the skies,
And to late times with blooming honours rise:
Whate'er th' unbounded Roman power obeys,
All climes and nations shall record my praise:
If 'tis allowed to poets to divine,
One half of round eternity is mine.

(trans. Leonard Welsted)

# from Tristia ('Sorrows')

## 3.10

*Ovid describes life in Tomis.*

If any yet do think of Naso's name,
Which yet within the city doth remain,
Know that I live within a barbarous land,
Which near unto the Northern Pole does stand.
The Sauromates and Getes do hem me in,
Whose ruder names my verse do not beseem.
While th' air is warm, we then defended are
By Isther, whose fair stream keeps back the war.
But when that Boreas once did fly abroad,
Those countries he with heavy snow does load.
Nor doth the snow dissolve by sun or rain,
But the North Wind doth make it still remain;
New snow doth fall on that which fell before,
While that the earth is doubly covered o'er.
Such is the North Wind's force when it doth blow,
That towers and houses it doth overthrow.
  The freezing mob short coats and mantles wear,
To guard their faces from the sullen air.
From their long hair a rustling sound is heard,
And hoary frost shines on each icy beard.
The fragrant wine to ice substantial turns,
Nor longer now in purple channels runs.
What should I here of frozen rivers tell,
Or waters dug from pits as deep as hell?
For Isther here with Nile may equal be,
Whose sev'nfold streams sink in the raging sea.
His azure waves hid o'er with ice he keeps,
And so unseen into the ocean creeps;
Where ships did fail, the labouring horses tread,

107

And on the river find an icy bed;
Sarmatian oxen draw their waggons o'er
Arches of ice stretched wide from shore to shore.
'Tis strange, yet true, but this as fact regard,
Since fictions here can bring me no reward,
We've seen the ocean crusted o'er with ice,
And the sea bound with frozen fetters twice.
Dry on the ocean's breast we often walk,
And there, as in some pleasant meadows, talk.
Had bold Leander such a shore descried,
The lover ne'er had in the ocean died.
The crooked dolphins cannot here repair
To the sea's verge to suck the balmy air.
And though the winds with all their fury blow,
No storms the seas or rising billows know.
No vessels there upon the billows ride,
No well-played oars the heavy waves divide.
The scaly fish, in icy fetters bound,
Upon the beach half-dead are often found,
If surly Boreas with too-powerful force
Stagnates the sea, and stops the rivers' course.
   When Isther by dry whirlwinds is congealed,
No longer then the foe can be concealed,
Who skilful in their horsemanship and bow,
Waste all around where'er their armies go.
The peasants fly, and none defend their fields,
Whilst their poor stock some little pillage yields.
Their riches is their cattle, and their wains,
And some mean wealth which their low cots contains.
Some by the barbarous foe when captive took,
Leave their dear earth with many a heavy look.
Others struck deep by barbèd arrows die,
Whose poisoned heads with wingèd vengeance fly.
What they can't take maliciously, they spoil,

And with hot flames their icy gods defile.
The fearful swain, for fear of being killed,
Neglected leaves his widowed farm untilled.
Not here the grapes hang in a leafy shade,
Nor is their wine from purple clusters made.
Acontius here could not an apple find,
To write his passion, and disclose his mind.
Her naked fields see no returning spring,
Nor on the trees the cheerful birds do sing.
And though the world hath such a large extent,
Here only I must suffer banishment.

(trans. T. P.)

# Glossary of Mythological and Historical Persons and Places

ACHILLES, son of Peleus; the most formidable Greek hero
   at the siege of Troy; his mother had tried to prevent
   him from going to the Trojan War by disguising him in
   girl's clothing; her deceit was discovered by Ulysses; at
   Achilles' death, a dispute arose between Ajax and
   Ulysses about who should inherit his arms.

ACONTIUS, the lover of Cydippe; he wrote upon an apple,
   'I swear by Diana to marry Acontius'; Cydippe found
   the apple, read the inscription, and was thus bound by
   the oath.

AEGINA, the daughter of Asophus; ravished by Jupiter,
   who had turned himself into fire.

AEOLUS, god of the winds.

AGAMEMNON, king of Argos; son of Atreus, and leader of
   the Greeks at the siege of Troy.

AJAX (AIAS), Greek warrior at the siege of Troy renowned
   for his brawn rather than his intelligence; when the
   arms of Achilles were awarded to Ulysses, he went mad
   with resentment and killed himself; after his death a
   hyacinth arose from the ground, its petals inscribed 'ai,
   ai', after the hero's name.

ALCIDES: Hercules (see PHILOCTETES).

AMPHITRYON, husband of Alcmena, with whom Jupiter
   slept in Amphitryon's guise.

ANTIOPE, daughter of Nycteus; violated by Jupiter in the
   form of a satyr.

APOLLO, god of healing, music, archery and light;
   identified by Ovid with Helios, the sun-god, who
   drives his chariot daily from east to west across the sky;

Apollo was the son of Jupiter, and had temples at Claros in Ionia, at Patara in Lydia, and on the island of Tenedos; his major oracle was at Delphi.

ARDEA, Latin city, besieged by Tarquin, king of Rome.

ARIADNE: see THESEUS.

ARNÈ, daughter of Aeolus; ravished by Neptune, disguised as a bull.

ASTERIA, a maiden carried away by Jupiter in the form of an eagle.

ATREUS: see AGAMEMNON.

AUGUSTUS, the first Roman emperor, formerly Octavian (see Chronology).

AURORA, goddess of dawn and wife of Tithonus, for whom she obtained immortality but forgot to ask also for eternal youth, with the result that he perpetually aged; Aurora also had an adulterous liaison with the mortal Cephalus.

AUSONIA, Italy (a poeticism).

BACCHANTES: see BACCHUS.

BACCHUS, god of wine, often represented as accompanied and/or worshipped by frenzied female votaries (Maenads or Bacchantes) or by satyrs.

BOREAS, the North Wind.

CAESAR, GAIUS JULIUS, Roman general and statesman, assassinated in 44 BC; Augustus was his adopted son.

CENTAURS, race of mythological creatures with the body and legs of a horse but the chest, head and arms of a man.

CERES, goddess of agriculture and mother of Proserpina, who was snatched away by Pluto to be queen of the Underworld.

CIMMERIANS, according to Homer, a people living in perpetual darkness at the edge of the world.

CLEOPATRA, Egyptian queen, mistress to Julius Caesar and

later to Mark Antony, with whom she was defeated by Octavian at the battle of Actium (31 BC).

CORINNA, name given by Ovid to his mistress in *Amores*; probably a fictional construct, rather than an historical personage.

CUPID: childlike god of love, son of Venus and Vulcan; depicted with wings and a quiverful of arrows, with which he afflicts his victims.

CYCLOPES (singular CYCLOPS), one-eyed giants who were said to have made Jupiter's thunderbolts.

CYLLENE, a mountain in Arcadia.

CYNTHIA, Diana.

CYTHEREA, Venus, who was said to have been born from the sea-foam near the island of Cythera.

DAEDALUS: see THESEUS.

DANAË, maiden from Argos; ravished by Jupiter in a shower of gold; mother of Perseus.

DECIUS, Publius Decius, a colleague of Mark Antony's, taken prisoner by Octavian in the battle at Mutina, but allowed to return to Antony, as a gesture of reconciliation.

DEOIS, Proserpina, daughter of Jupiter, but ravished by him.

DIANA, goddess of the moon, childbirth, hunting and virginity.

DICTEAN, Cretan.

DRYADS, tree-nymphs.

ELYSIUM, part of the Underworld.

ENDYMION, beautiful youth, beloved of the Moon.

EURYDICE: see ORPHEUS.

FURIES, goddess-like spirits who avenge crimes done against kindred; represented as carrying torches and whips, and wreathed with snakes.

GETES (GETAE), a tribe at Tomis.

HAMADRYADS, tree-nymphs.

HELEN: see LEDA.

HESPERIAN, relating to the Hesperides, maidens who guarded a mythical tree producing golden apples.

HIPPODAMIA, wife of Pirithous, king of the Lapiths; her wedding-feast was interrupted by the riotous behaviour of the centaurs.

IDA: (1) a range of mountains near Troy where the Trojan prince Paris was brought up as a shepherd (it having been predicted that he would destroy his city); (2) mountain in the centre of Crete, the scene of Pasiphaë's encounter with the bull.

IO, maiden beloved of Jupiter, and transformed into a cow to conceal the affair from Juno.

ISTHER, the river Danube.

JOVE, Jupiter.

JUNO, wife of Jupiter, of whose numerous extra-marital affairs she frequently displayed vindictive jealousy.

JUPITER, king of the gods, and dispenser of justice by means of thunder and lightning; also the lecherous seducer of numerous mortal maidens.

LAIS, a celebrated Corinthian courtesan.

LEANDER, mythical lover who swam the Hellespont to visit his beloved Hero.

LEDA, Spartan queen, impregnated by Jupiter in the form of a swan; their daughter, Helen, married Menelaus, king of Sparta; Paris abducted her, thus causing the Trojan War.

LETHE, river of forgetfulness in the Underworld.

LUCIFER, the morning star.

LYCAON, a mythical king of Arcadia.

MAENALUS, a mountain range in Arcadia.

MARS, god of war; lover of Venus.

MEDUSA, the snake-haired Gorgon, from whose blood the winged horse Pegasus sprang.

MEMNON, son of Aurora; he fought on the Trojan side in the siege of Troy, and was killed by Achilles; each year his grave was said to be visited by birds sprung from his ashes.

MEMPHIS, city in Lower Egypt.

MERCURY, messenger of the gods, particularly Jupiter; depicted with a herald's staff, and winged hat and shoes.

METHYMNA, a city near the shore of the island of Lesbos.

MILO, a famous wrestler and athlete.

MINERVA, Roman equivalent of the Greek Pallas Athene, goddess of war, spinning and weaving, and wisdom.

MINOS: see THESEUS.

MINOTAUR: see THESEUS.

MNEMOSYNE, a maiden ravished by Jupiter, in the guise of a shepherd; mother of the Muses.

MUSES, the nine goddesses presiding over the arts and other intellectual pursuits, seen by artists as their principal source of inspiration.

MUTINA, a city in Cisalpine Gaul, site of a battle between Octavian and Mark Antony in 43 BC.

NAIADS, nymphs of springs, rivers and lakes.

NEPTUNE, god of the sea.

NEREIDS, sea-maidens, the daughters of the sea-god Nereus.

NESTOR, king of Pylos; the oldest of the Greek warriors at Troy; wise, but garrulous and anecdotal.

OCTAVIAN: see AUGUSTUS.

ORPHEUS, Thracian poet and lyre-player, able to charm wild beasts, and even rocks and trees, with his songs; his wife Eurydice was bitten by a snake; Orpheus descended to the Underworld to recover her and was allowed to take her back with him, but only on condition that he did not look back; he did so, and Eurydice was thus lost for ever.

PALAMEDE(S), a Greek hero who, when Ulysses tried to avoid going to Troy by pretending to be mad, exposed his deceit; in revenge, Ulysses fabricated evidence which suggested that Palamedes was a traitor, as a result of which Palamedes was stoned to death.

PALLAS, Minerva.

PAN, god of shepherds and flocks; in Ovid, a crude, rustic singer.

PANDION, king of Athens, and father of Procne and Philomela.

PARNASSUS, mountain north of Delphi, associated with Apollo and the Muses.

PASIPHAË: see THESEUS.

PELEUS: see ACHILLES.

PENEUS, a Thessalian river-god.

PHAETHON, son of Apollo.

PHARSALIA, scene of the defeat of Pompey by Julius Caesar in 48 BC.

PHILIPPI, scene of defeat of Brutus and Cassius by Mark Antony and Octavian in 42 BC.

PHILOCTETES, Greek warrior; the inheritor of Hercules' mighty bow and arrows; bitten by a snake on the way to Troy, and abandoned on the island of Lemnos at the instigation of Ulysses; later persuaded by Ulysses to return to the siege, where (as predicted) his weapons proved invaluable in securing the Greek victory.

PHOEBUS, epithet for Apollo.

PLUTO, god of the Underworld.

POMPEY, Roman general, the opponent of Julius Caesar in the Roman civil war which began in 49 BC; defeated by

Caesar at Pharsalia; his son Sextus Pompeius was defeated by Mark Antony in 36 BC.

PROMETHEUS, a Titan who, according to some legends, moulded the first men and women from clay.

PROSERPINA: see CERES.

PYLIAN: see NESTOR.

PYTHON, a serpent, slain by Apollo at Delphi.

QUIRINUS: see ROMULUS.

ROMULUS, one of the legendary founders of Rome, said to have secured brides for his people by encouraging them to carry off the wives of the Sabines, a neighbouring tribe; later worshipped by the Romans as Quirinus.

SATURN, the father of Jupiter.

SATYRS: attendants of Bacchus; represented as half human, and half horse or goat; lustful and riotous.

SAUROMATES, Sarmatians (a tribe at Tomis).

SIDONIAN, Phoenician.

SILENUS, drunken rustic god often associated with the satyrs.

SISYPHUS: see ULYSSES.

STYX, principal river of the Underworld; an oath by the Styx was held by the gods to be inviolable.

TANTALUS, a Lydian king, punished in the Underworld for offences against the gods by being perpetually in the proximity of food and drink which he was prevented from tasting.

TARPEIAN ROCK, rock at the south-west corner of the Capitoline Hill in Rome, from which condemned criminals were hurled.

THESEUS, Athenian hero; among his many exploits was the killing of the Minotaur, a monster, half bull and half man, the result of the union between Pasiphaë, wife of Minos, king of Crete, and a bull; Minos hid the Minotaur in the Labyrinth, a maze constructed by the

Athenian craftsman Daedalus, and forced the Athenians to pay a regular tribute of youths and maidens, who were shut up in the Labyrinth; Ariadne, Minos' daughter, fell in love with Theseus and helped him kill the Minotaur and escape from Crete, but she was then abandoned by Theseus on the island of Naxos.

THESSALY, area of Greece renowned as the home of sorcerers.

TIPHYS, helmsman of the *Argo*, in which Jason sailed to Colchis to gain the golden Fleece.

TOMIS, remote and barbaric settlement on the Black Sea, to which Ovid was banished in AD 8 (see Chronology).

ULYSSES, the most quick-witted and devious of the Greek warriors at Troy; said by some to be the son of the cunning trickster Sisyphus; accused by Ajax of cowardice and duplicity, he claimed that his intellect and cunning had achieved more for the Greeks than Ajax's mindless physical courage.

VENUS, love-goddess; lover of Mars; mother of the Trojan prince Aeneas and hence (since Rome was said to have been founded by Aeneas' descendants) patron goddess of Rome.

VESTALS, virgins whose duty it was to watch the fire in the temple of Vesta, Roman goddess of the hearth and family.

XANTHUS, one of the rivers on the plains of Troy.

# Chronology of Ovid's Life

| Year | Life |
|---|---|
| 44 BC | |
| 43 BC | 20 Mar. Ovid (Publius Ovidius Naso) born at Sulmo on the Abruzzi, the son of an old equestrian family. |
| ?37 BC | |
| 31 BC | |
| 30 BC | |
| 29 BC | |
| 29–19 BC | |
| 28 BC | |
| 27 BC | |
| c. 27 BC | Ovid assumes the toga with the 'broad purple stripe', a sign that he was a candidate for the *cursus honorum*, the sequence of magistracies leading to admission to the Senate. |
| ?c. 25 BC | Ovid begins work on *Amores* ('Loves'). |

# Chronology of his Times

| Year | Cultural Context | Historical Context |
|---|---|---|
| 44 BC | | 13 Mar. Assassination of Julius Caesar. The publication of Caesar's will reveals that Octavian has been adopted as his heir. |
| 43 BC | | c. 27 Apr. Octavian defeats Mark Antony at the battle of Mutina. Octavian and Antony subsequently reconciled. |
| | | 27 Nov. Establishment of triumvirate (Octavian, Mark Antony, Lepidus) to rule Rome and the Empire. |
| ?37 BC | Publication of Virgil's *Eclogues*. Around this date, Virgil joins the circle of Maecenas and Octavian. | |
| 31 BC | | Octavian assumes the consulship and defeats Antony and Cleopatra at the Battle of Actium (13 Sept.). |
| 30 BC | Publication of Horace, *Satires*, 1. | |
| 29 BC | Publication of Virgil's *Georgics*. | |
| 29–19 BC | Composition of Virgil's *Aeneid*. | |
| 28 BC | Octavian's Mausoleum, gardens and crematorium built on the Campus Martius. | |
| 27 BC | Building work starts on the Pantheon in the Campus Martius. | 16 Jan. Octavian receives the title Augustus, thus affirming his superior position in the Senate. |
| c. 27 BC | | |
| ?c. 25 BC | | |

| Year | Life |
|------|------|
| after 24 BC | Ovid embarks on a career in public service. |
| 23 BC | |
| 20 BC | |
| 19 BC | |
| 18–17 BC | |
| not before 16 BC | The revised *Amores*, in three books, published. |
| 13 BC | |
| 12 BC | |
| 8 BC | |
| by 2 BC | |
| ? before 2 BC | Composition of *Heroides* ('Letters of the Heroines') 1–14. |
| 2 BC | |
| ?2 BC–AD1 | Publication of *Ars amatoria* ('The Art of Love'). |
| 2 BC–AD2 | Publication of *Remedia amoris* ('Remedies for Love'). |
| ?AD 1–8 | Composition of *Heroides* 16–21. |
| AD 4 | |
| before AD 8 | Composition of *Metamorphoses* ('Transformations'), Ovid's most famous work. From the same period comes *Fasti* ('The Calendar'). |
| AD 8 | Ovid exiled to Tomis. |

| Year | Cultural Context | Historical Context |
|---|---|---|
| after 24 BC | | |
| 23 BC | Publication of Horace, *Odes* 1–3. Virgil reads Books 2, 4 and 6 of the *Aeneid* to Augustus' family. | Death of Marcellus (Augustus' son-in-law and heir-apparent). 23 July. Augustus resigns the consulship but is granted powers involving complete control of the Senate, a move which marks the absolute end of the Roman Republic. |
| 20 BC | Publication of Horace, *Epistles* 1. | |
| 19 BC | Deaths of Virgil and Tibullus. | |
| 18–17 BC | | Augustus introduces a programme of moral and religious reform. |
| not before 16 BC | Publication of Propertius, *Elegies* 4. | |
| 13 BC | ?Publication of Horace, *Odes*, 4. | |
| 12 BC | | Augustus becomes Pontifex Maximus (the official head of Roman religion). |
| 8 BC | 27 Nov. Death of Horace. Death of Maecenas. | |
| ?before 2 BC | | |
| 2 BC | Dedication of the Forum of Augustus, containing the temple of Mars Ultor ('Mars the Avenger'). | Augustus saluted as *Pater Patriae*. His daughter Julia banished for adultery. |
| ?2 BC–AD 1 | | |
| 2 BC–AD 2 | | |
| ?AD 1–8 | | |
| AD 4 | | Tiberius adopted by Augustus as his likely successor. |
| before AD 8 | | |
| AD 8 | | Augustus' granddaughter Julia banished for adultery. |

| Year | Life |
|------|------|
| AD 9 | |
| AD 9–12 | *Tristia* ('Sorrows') sent from Ovid in exile to his wife and to (unnamed) Roman friends. |
| c. AD 10 | Composition of *Ibis*, an abstruse curse-poem, directed against an unnamed enemy. |
| AD 13 | Publication of *Epistulae ex Ponto* ('Letters from Pontus') 1–3. |
| AD 14 | |
| AD 17 | Death of Ovid at Tomis. |

| Year | Cultural Context | Historical Context |
|---|---|---|
| AD 9 | | Augustus' last social law, the *Lex Papia Poppaea*, offering further inducements to have children. |
| AD 9–12 | | |
| c. AD 10 | | |
| AD 13 | | |
| AD 14 | | 9 Aug. Death of Augustus. 17 Sept. Tiberius proclaimed Emperor. |
| AD 17 | Death of Livy. | |